FRANCHISING
Is It Fair ?

How To Negotiate An
Equitable Franchise
Agreement

Jay S. Patel

President and CEO,
Lodging Hospitality Systems, Inc.

Copyright © 1999 by Jay S. Patel

Published by Coco Design Associates, Inc.
ISBN 1-57635-054-1
Franchising: Is It Fair?
An imprint of We Write Corporation
P.O. Box 644, Rochester, Illinois 62563

Printed in the United States of America

For more information contact:
Amerifirst Network
2400 W. Michigan Avenue—Suite 17A
Pensacola, Florida 32526

info@isitfair.com
http://isitfair.com

Library of Congress Cataloging-in-Publication Data

EXPERT TESTIMONY

Enlightened franchisors understand that their franchise agreements are partnership agreements of trust between the franchisee and franchisor. Unfortunately, too many hotel franchising agreements, particularly those offered by the more powerful brands, are skewed in favor of the franchisor. They contain as many rights and as few responsibilities as possible for franchisors, while just the opposite is true for franchisees. This franchisor favoritism should surprise no one because high-paid franchisor attorneys offer 100% protection to the franchisor against any and all contingencies including lawsuits.

Jay S. Patel has courageously written *How to Negotiate an Equitable Franchise Agreement.* Every potential franchisee should read this book before signing their franchise agreement. Jay Patel has provided an incredible resource to help address the unfavorable imbalance between hotel franchisees who deliver high quality and guest value and powerful hotel franchisors who want to continue the status quo.

His book offers no-nonsense practical tips on how to negotiate the elimination of personal guarantees, onerous liquidated damages provisions and restrictions on the sale of the franchise. This is a must-read book for hotel students, franchisors and franchisees who seek an industry solution to fair franchising.

Robert C. Hazard Jr.
Chairman, Creative Hotel Associates
Former Chairman & CEO, Choice Hotels International, Inc.

Jay Patel has done a service not only to hotel owners but to the entire franchise industry by authoring this book. The lodging industry in particular owes him a debt of gratitude for tackling a tough topic and dealing with it in a straightforward and candid manner.

Important tips he's given on the various aspects of franchise agreements will go a long way towards helping those who no longer want to leave to chance those issues that will be the basis upon which a franchisee's financial success rests.

This is a must read for anyone who derives their livelihood from the hospitality industry.

Robert Nozar, Editor in Chief
Hotel & Motel Management Magazine

This book will sweep the franchise industry! Jay Patel has carefully provided the reader a chance to explore the world of franchise contract negotiations that is so wonderfully obvious and incredibly basic you'll find it hard to believe that's all there is to it! And when you are done, you will find yourself inspired and motivated because you now know more about the way you do business whether you are a franchisor or a franchisee.

We are grateful to Jay for taking this brave step in sharing his learnings. In *Franchising: Is it Fair?*, Jay has done an outstanding job to ensure that franchisees will protect their assets and move a step closer to a more fruitful relationship with their franchisors.

Mike Patel, Chairman, Industry Relations
Committee and 1998 Chairman, Asian
American Hotel Owners Association (AAHOA)

In a world of inequitable franchise contracts it becomes essential to choose a good business partner. Fortunately, Jay Patel has developed a comprehensive guide for both current and prospective franchisees in *How to Negotiate an Equitable Franchise Agreement*. The book discusses everything from basic franchise contracts to franchisee estate planning.

By exposing the inequities which are abundant throughout franchise contracts, Patel shows the reader a way out. He steers the reader from the typical risk intensive franchisee position to, essentially, a more equitable partnership position.

While looking over the next franchise contract remember the useful advice that Jay Patel shares, and take comfort in knowing that you now have an insider's guide to help you through the process.

Stephen Rushmore, Founder and President
Hospitality Valuation Services

Jay Patel's combination of talent and experience has produced a rare book, *Franchising: Is it Fair? How to Negotiate an Equitable Franchise Agreement*, ideal for the entrepreneur who has very little time to learn a lot about franchise negotiating, encroachment, dispute resolution, advertising fund agreements, etc.

Franchise owners have, for many years, tried to find a level playing field but seldom make significant progress. Jay's book shortens their learning curve and is useful not only for franchisees but also for franchise company personnel as well.

As the 1999 Chairman of AAHOA, and on behalf of the 5,000 members I represent, we congratulate Jay Patel for his unselfish efforts in providing this invaluable reference tool for franchisees all over the world. This is a guide no franchisee should be without.

Ramesh Surati, 1999 Chairman,
Asian American Hotel Owners Association (AAHOA)

We are thrilled to be able to bring a book to our members that offers great insight into the art of negotiating a franchise agreement. I look forward to sharing this book entitled *How to Negotiate an Equitable Franchise Agreement* with our AAHOA members. This book will be a tremendous help to anyone interested in boosting his or her knowledge of franchising. They say knowledge is power. There is no doubt that after reading this book, a prospective franchisee will have the power to negotiate a better contract. This book should be required reading for anyone who wants to strengthen their knowledge and ability in franchise negotiation.

Fred Schwartz
Executive Director
Asian American Hotel Owners Association (AAHOA)

CONTENTS

Acknowledgements

M y sincere thanks to God for this opportunity to share all that I have learned over the years about the franchise industry. If each person who reads this book can change just one provision in their new or successive franchise contracts, then my effort will have been worthwhile.

I also wish to thank the following franchise attorneys for their assistance in researching and reviewing the entire manuscript (in alphabetical order): Brent R. Appel, Esq.; Marc Blumenthal, Esq.; Patrick Carter, Esq.; Carmen D. Caruso, P.C.; Harris J. Chernow, Esq.; Michael Dady, Esq.; Michael Einbinder, Esq.; Eric Karp, Esq.; Peter Lagarias, Esq.; Michael R. Liss, Esq.; Gerald A. Marks, Esq.; John Martland, Esq.; Kenneth A. Rutherford, Esq.; Andrew Selden, Esq.; Peter A. Singler Jr., Esq.; Joseph Thomson, Esq.; and Robert Zarco, Esq.

(A complete list of recommended franchise attorneys with addresses and telephone numbers are included on pages 139–143 in the back of this book.)

I also want to recognize and thank the American Franchisee Association's (AFA) President, Susan P. Kezios for the personal leadership she undertakes on behalf of all franchisees in the pursuit of their legal and constitutional rights. The AFA's Director of Public Policy, Samuel J. Crawford, is also to be commended for his assistance to me in locating information utilized in writing this book.

The AAHOA Board of Directors deserves a thank you for their friendship and advise as I embarked on this project (in alphabetical order): Ashokkumar Ranchhod, Asvin Patel, A. V. Patel, Balvant (Bill) Patel, Bakulesh (Buggsi) Patel,

Bhavesh (Bobby) Patel, Bharat V. Patel, Bhupen S. Patel, Chandra I. (C. K.) Patel, Chandrakant M. Patel, Chandu Z. Patel, Chhotalal B. Patel, Dahyabhai V. Patel, Dhansukh (Dan) Patel, Dinubhai Patel, Diru (Robin) Prema, Fred Schwartz, Hashmukh R. Patel, Hitesh Patel, Jay Patel, J. P. Rama, Mahendra P. Patel, Mahesh (Mike) Amin, Manu Patel, Mike Patel, Narendra (Naz) Patel, Naresh (Nash) Patel, Prabhu M. Patel, Pragna Patel, Pratik A. Chauhan, Priti Patel, Rajesh (Roger) Leva, Ramesh Surati, Richard Reyer, Rohit Patel, Salim Manji, Saroj Patel, Vijay K. Sethi and the rest of the AAHOA Staff.

And I cannot forget to mention the members of the AAHOA Industry Relations Committee who first inspired me to begin the journey to put these thoughts down on paper (in alphbetical order): Asvin Patel, Bharat Patel, Bobby Patel, C. N. Patel, Hitesh Bhakta, Mahesh Patel, Mike Patel, Andrew Selden, Ramesh Surati and Ravi Patel.

The executive staff at Lodging Hospitality Systems gave me the space and time I needed to complete this book. I want to thank Nash Patel, Neil Patel, Vishal Patel, Zonya Martinez, Kandace Diamond, Suzanne Fiola and the rest of my staff for their help.

I take my hat off to my good friends Jay Massey and Joe Martin at Coco Design Associates of Pensacola, Florida, who designed and published this book.

With much respect and love I acknowledge my wife, two children and my mother for their patience and understanding as I worked too, too, too many hours bringing this project to completion.

And finally, I owe a debt of gratitude to everyone who has touched my life with inspiration and many unforgettable experiences but who are too numerous to name. I have learned much from each and every one of you.

Jay Patel, President
Lodging Hospitality Systems, Inc.
August 1999

Foreword

Those of us who work in franchising find ourselves at a unique crossroad. We are poised at the start of a new century and we have come to a fork in the road. One path leads us down the same old dusty road franchising has been traveling, where we watch certain franchisors abuse their franchisees through arbitrary and unilateral actions. The other path leads us onto a new thoroughfare where we choose to level the playing field between franchisors and franchisees through more equitable franchise contracts.

The only way to level the playing field is by enacting baseline standards of conduct for franchisors and franchisees to abide by after the franchise sale has been made. Currently, there are no federal laws requiring franchisors and franchisees to abide by the common law duty of good faith in their dealings with each other; no duty of due care that the franchisor must show to its franchisees; no limited fiduciary duty when the franchisor handles its franchisees' money in bookkeeping or accounting functions or pooled advertising funds. In other words, there are no rules in the franchise game—other than what the franchisor writes into the franchise contract and presents to the franchisee on a take-it-or-leave-it basis.

So what do you do in the meantime? Because of the unequal bargaining power between a franchisor and franchisee, one of the only ways you can protect yourself is by reading this book. Author Jay Patel advocates understanding the potential for abuse within a franchise contract and offers suggestions on ways you might negotiate around those abuses. Jay's effort is long overdue. Most books about franchising advise readers to "investigate before investing" but never really give you the nuts-and-bolts questions to ask and the pitfalls to avoid as Jay does in *Franchising: Is it Fair?*

No, in today's world, franchising is not fair. Today's franchise contract is often written in a manner that is fundamentally unfair to the franchisee. And even if many or most franchisors do not abuse their position and power and even if some franchisees are large and sophisticated investors, we still need federal laws to discourage franchise abuses and books like Jay Patel's to inform and enlighten potential franchise investors.

So, which road do you want to walk in the 21st century? The old, dusty one with franchisors who write contracts that give franchising a black eye? Or the new thoroughfare with more equitable franchise contracts and more satisfactory franchise relationships between franchisors and franchisees?

I know which road Jay Patel and I will travel. How about you?

Susan P. Kezios
President
American Franchisee Association (AFA)

INTRODUCTION

This book is written for businesspeople, not lawyers. Specifically, it is written for those who are either buying a franchise for the first time or who are renewing their existing franchise agreement. The information is meant to provide practical, real-life advice. Franchise agreements are not like any other legal document. They are unique, novel and initially intimidating to most businesspeople and also to many lawyers. Renewing franchisees especially are shocked by the drastically different terms that change the financial and operational benefits of owning a franchise for them and their families.

Lawyers for franchisors are including all sorts of new provisions that do nothing but oppress the franchisee investor. Franchisors are now attempting to get consent in advance for every tactic they use in these so-called state-of-the-art franchise agreements.

A good attorney friend of mine attended a predominantly franchisor lawyer-attended legal symposium some time ago. One of the seminars was on the subject of encroachment, which certain franchisors insist on calling "system expansion" in an effort to mask the consequences of their sometimes predatory actions in this area. Two rather startling things occurred at this seminar.

First, one of the presenters, in an effort to lead with humor, said substantially the following: "In planning for this presentation, we thought we might use a title like 'How To Put up a New Unit Across the Street from Your Franchisee and Get Away with It.' But that would be a bit obvious. So instead, we decided to use the title 'System Expansion'."

The attorneys in the room who primarily represented franchisees and their independent associations were not laughing. Franchisor lawyers thought it was a great joke. If what the comedian Alan King once said is true, that the root of all great humor is truth, then the reader understands what franchisees are up against when entering into franchise contracts.

Second, at a different seminar at this same legal symposium, the general counsel for one of the country's largest franchisors, in response to a discussion about the wisdom and the impact of the then-recently issued Scheck decision, made his view very clear—no judge, federal or state, was going to tell him where he could or could not develop a unit. The arrogance of that remark and the gross imbalance of legal and economic power in the franchise relationship point to the urgent need for meaningful change in franchising.

Franchisors go to any lengths to develop contracts that protect their business interests. The purpose of franchising is to allow individuals to enter into the established business operations of franchisors to achieve a mutually beneficial relationship in an entrepreneurial environment. This can be accomplished only if both parties act in good faith, deal fairly and honestly and are able to rely on each other.

It is very important that a person seeking to purchase a new or existing franchise utilize the information contained in this book. Use the tips it contains to guide your negotiating process. All franchisors will state that they do not negotiate the contents of their franchise agreements. But if you hold firm to equitable reasoning and act ready to walk away from the deal, there is a chance the franchisor will consider negotiating. And if not, make good on your threat, do business elsewhere and tell your friends to do business elsewhere, too.

I have been accused of being an advocate against the franchise industry, especially now that I am also a franchisor. In the early 90s, when I started to play an active role with such organizations as the Indo American Hospitality Association (IAHA) and the Asian American Hotel Owners Association (AAHOA), I got involved with franchising hotels. As I started to understand the true nature of how franchising worked, I realized there was sufficient reason for concern over the predatory, opportunistic and often abusive practices of some franchisors.

Lack of education has been the pitfall for many franchisees. While they spend endless time on the operational success of their investments, they spend little or no time understanding the agreements they sign with franchisors. Often, they leave it to their local attorneys who have little or no franchise experience. This lack of knowledge in combination with ill-placed trust in the "standard franchise agreement" leads to franchise agreements that are extremely one-sided and basically presented to franchisees on a take-it-or-leave-it basis.

It astonished me when I learned that the Federal Trade Commission (FTC), the only regulatory body overseeing franchising, stated it "does not have the resources to follow up on all meritorious complaints" filed by franchisees. Franchisors tout that the franchise industry today employs more than eight million workers in over a half million small businesses in more than 60 different industries. Combined annual sales of these franchised businesses account for more than one-third of all retail sales of goods and services in the United States. Franchising gets larger and larger, the complaints continue to flow, but the only federal agency charged with its oversight states they cannot follow up on "all meritorious complaints." Something is terribly wrong.

It is my opinion, and some shall agree, that the franchise industry has been tarnished by a few bad actor franchisors. There are, however, some franchisors that respect and promote the investment interests of their franchisees. Which ones are sincere? Only actual franchisees can answer that question.

The purpose of this book is to first, educate franchisees on what they commit to when they sign franchise agreements and, second, to motivate franchisors to be reasonable, factual and fair in administering their franchise systems. As Bill Clinton repeated often during one of his campaigns for the U.S. presidency, "People who work hard and play by the rules should not be punished, but should share in the reward for the American Dream." Nowhere is the President's vision for change more urgently needed than in today's franchise agreements.

CHAPTER I
FRANCHISE AGREEMENTS

Negotiate: How and Why

Negotiating a franchise agreement for both first-time and renewing franchisees is far more effective when both the franchisor and franchisee have knowledge and awareness of the process. The goal is threefold: to increase the franchisee's knowledge of what the franchise agreement really says; to increase the franchisee's awareness of whether or not the franchisor really wants to subjugate its franchisees to onerous contractual provisions; and to assist the franchisee in determining whether or not there is mutual respect from the franchisor to its franchisees.

Undertaken with these thoughts in mind, the process of negotiating the franchise agreement should enlighten the franchisee. Is this the kind of person he/she wants as their franchisor? Is this the kind of person he/she wants as their leader and mentor? Eventually a franchisee's knowledge will benefit his/her franchisor as well, leading to a stronger overall franchise program. Weak, ill-informed franchisees ultimately lead to weak overall franchise programs.

Franchise negotiations cannot be looked at as a zero-sum game in which for each negotiated contract provision one side wins and the other side loses. If that win-lose mentality is applied at the outset of the franchise relationship or to the proposed renewal of the franchise, then it spells doom to the upcoming multi-year relationship—especially from the franchisee's standpoint. A franchisor who at the very start tries to win more with the end result of his/her franchisees losing more is missing the original intent of using franchising as a method of distributing products and/or services to the public. For franchising to work it must be win-win. It must be a relationship that is mutually beneficial to both the franchisor and the franchisee. Greed must not rear its ugly head with the end result being the enslavement of the franchisee. The franchisee who allows him/herself to be enslaved is unlikely to be the kind of business partner the franchisor would want in the franchise system anyway.

> *The franchisor's own staff may be appalled once they are actually shown what the agreement says and what it means.*

Franchisees and franchisors must learn what the proposed contract terms say and discern what they mean for the long-term health of their eventual business relationship. The knowledgeable franchise buyer who is aware of what the proposed agreement terms mean may decide it is important to balance the relationship by removing the more asymmetrical, totally one-sided, pro-franchisor paragraphs. The franchise buyer should be ready to say, "Deal with me fairly or I will not do business with you."

The franchisor's own staff as well as its senior executives may be appalled once they are shown what the franchise agreement says and learn what it means from a business perspective. All too often, the franchise agreement has been prepared by a franchisor lawyer who, acting to protect the client, loads it up with every pro-franchisor paragraph available. Inevitably this makes the franchise agreement anti-franchisee. A franchisor's business personnel have not really had to deal with the fine print in the agreement to determine if it really is a reflection of their company's policies and how they want to treat their franchisees. In fact, many franchisor personnel, once they are made aware of what certain franchise agreement terms mean and what they imply about the kind of company they are, direct their franchise lawyer to make changes which will more closely reflect their business policies. They have concluded that if they were buying one of their own franchises, they would not sign an agreement with similar provisions, so how can they ask franchise buyers to sign them? Smart businesspeople live in the world of win-win, not win-lose.

> *Too often, the franchise agreement was prepared by a franchisor lawyer who loaded it up with every pro-franchisor paragraph available.*

Purchasers of franchises have more power than they realize. As purchasers or investors in franchise systems, franchisees are the customers. All too often, franchisees assume they cannot change their franchise agreements. They take a defeatist attitude, not even asking for changes. But franchisees should remember, "if you don't ask for it, you can't get it." Franchisees must also remember how eagerly most franchisors want to sell franchises. Most franchisors are not large. Hundreds if not thousands of franchise chains have only a few dozen properties operating—and that is after trying to sell franchises for five to ten years. That means a franchisor may sell only one franchise every month or so. Therefore when the initial franchise buyer or the renewing franchisee comes along, that person is really a big fish. Franchisees get their attention. They will want to find a way to sell to them, even if it means changing some of that legal mumbo-jumbo in the franchise agreement. We are not talking about changing the business reality of the deal, i.e., the up-front franchise fee or the royalties to the franchisor. We are talking about changing the abusive legal terminology that attempts to enslave the franchisee to the franchisor. These provisions need changing to make the franchise agreement more equitable to both sides.

> *"If you don't ask for it, you can't get it."*

Obviously, if more than one franchisee asks for a contractual change, it is more meaningful to the franchisor. If 50 franchisees or 50 percent of franchisees within the same brand ask for the same contractual change, it gets the franchisor's attention. Getting franchisees together to ask the franchisor for contractual or operational changes is one of the most persuasive and effective ways to convince a reluctant franchisor to listen and actually deal with his/her customers. Sometimes this process is called collective bargaining. Sometimes franchisees form independent franchisee associations as a means to get together and cohesively communicate with the franchisor. Both channels are simply geared at balancing the relationship between the franchisor and franchisee as reflected in the written franchise agreement. This process is healthy both for the franchisor and for the franchise system as a whole.

Franchise statutes in a few states prohibit franchisors from directly or indirectly interfering in the formation of independent franchisee associations (Arkansas, California, Hawaii, Illinois, Iowa, Michigan, Minnesota, Nebraska, New Jersey, Rhode Island, Washington). These types of laws, although available in a limited number of states, are designed to protect both prospective and renewing franchisees' investments in their franchises.

> *"One of the strongest positions in negotiating comes from the ability to walk away from the deal."*

Timing and having adequate time are critical elements in the franchise negotiation process. One of the strongest positions in negotiating comes from the ability to walk away from the deal. This is true when negotiating to buy a new car and it is no less true when negotiating to buy a franchise. Realizing there are alternatives and allowing enough time to research and pursue them are necessary to the success of any negotiation. If a prospective franchisee is going to buy a particular franchise no matter what the franchisor does during the pre-sales process and if the franchisor perceives the franchisee will sign, then the franchisee has no bargaining power. The prospective franchisee must not appear overly eager. The prospectivre franchisee must play hard-to-get. In other words, the franchisor must believe, that if the franchisor does not make certain requested changes to the franchise agreement, there is a significant probability the prospective franchisee will buy a different franchise. This is true even when it comes time to renew an existing franchise agreement.

Adequate time to do something else—whether to buy a different franchise or buy nothing—is critical. Franchisees need to know they have adequate time so they do not feel trapped, so they do not feel there is no alternative and begin accepting all of the franchisor's demands. The franchisor needs to believe the prospective franchisee will really say, "no." With this knowledge, the franchisor is more likely to deal fairly. If however, the franchisor sees a franchisee trapped by time and who is overly eager, the franchisor will often just take advantage and say, "sign." That will be the beginning of the end for the new franchisee because it demonstrates the win-lose nature of that particular franchisor.

Too many times franchisees have heard, "There is another application submitted" or "Someone else is also inquiring on the brand."

Too many times franchisees have heard, "There is another application submitted," or "Someone else is also inquiring on the brand." This is not always true. It is often just a tactic used by franchise salespeople to create a false sense of urgency for the prospect to purchase the franchise. Franchisees must be very careful about purchasing a franchise before they have secured financing. Inquiring about the availability of a particular franchise is far different from actually purchasing. Too many franchisees have forfeited the initial deposit and been subject to liquidated damages for signing on the dotted line too quickly. When purchasing a franchise, the franchisee should have it put in writing that the initial fees shall be refunded if the financing does not come through.

With the right "can do" perspective and an experienced franchisee attorney, franchisees can take control of their destinies. It does no good to take a franchise agreement to the attorney after it has been signed. An attorney can negotiate the agreement so it reflects what both the franchisor and the franchisee want at the start of a business relationship. A franchisee must make it a win-win relationship from the start and be prepared to tell the franchisor there will be "no deal" otherwise.

The balance of this chapter will focus on examples of the pro-franchisor provisions imbedded in some franchise agreements. These are the provisions which must be identified in the agreement and either removed or modified so it makes business sense to both the franchisor and the franchisee.

Personal Guarantee

Virtually every franchisor is a corporation (or limited liability company) and for good reason. Ask the franchisor why the company is incorporated. Every reason provided is another reason why franchisees should also be incorporated. Limiting personal liability for business risks, facilitating multiple ownership, the appearance of professionalism, tax advantages . . . the list goes on and on. These are all good reasons for both franchisors and franchisees to incorporate. However, it is common for franchisors to require a personal signature or a personal guarantee from a franchisee on a corporate signature. Why? To tie franchisees' personal assets to the success or failure of the franchise.

Why the franchisor wants to sign the franchise agreement as a corporation . . . and why the franchisee should do the same.

Franchisors are likely to say the franchise agreement is like a promissory note to the bank. Actually, that reasoning is false because: (1) banks provide cash up front to franchisees while the franchisor does not. (Franchise agreements are simply pay-as-you-go agreements in which franchisees pay a royalty each month, typically on their gross sales.) (2) Many bank loans are made without personal guarantees when there is a good credit evaluation. Deep down, the reasons why the franchisor wants to sign the franchise agreement as a corporation, are the same reasons why the franchisee should do the same.

If a franchisee provides the franchisor with some personal guarantee, then he/she should attempt to limit it in any way possible. For example, the franchisee should have it only apply for the first (risky) years of the business or should have it apply for a limited amount of money, (i.e. six months of royalties). Also, the franchisee should have as few guarantors as possible. In a family business and/or partnership, for example, the franchisees should have just one spouse or partner listed as guarantor.

Transfer Issues

An important issue for any franchisee is the right to sell the franchise to a third party. The franchisor has a strong interest in such a transfer because he/she seeks to maintain the strength of its franchise system. Typically, franchise agreements contain various clauses that relate to the transfer of a franchise. These matters should be reviewed carefully and the franchisee should try to negotiate certain provisions to his/her favor.

Transfer fees charged by the franchisor must bear some relationship to his/her actual expenses upon the sale of the franchise.

Many franchise agreements provide that upon the transfer of a franchise the franchisee has to pay a transfer fee. The amount of the fee can range from a few hundred dollars to as much as many thousands or even tens of thousands of dollars. If the fee seems unreasonable, the franchisee should negotiate this clause before buying the franchise. It may be negotiable both at the execution of the franchise agreement and at the sale of the franchise. The transfer fees charged by the franchisor should bear some relationship to his/her actual expenses upon the sale of the franchise and any other fees incurred in connection with the franchise sale. For example, if the franchisor charges a franchise fee to a transferee that relates to training expenses, that may be a reasonable basis on which to base the transfer fee. On the other hand, if a transferee is an existing franchisee of the system, he/she may not require additional training. In this case, there should be no training fees. In negotiating these provisions, franchisees should ascertain the franchisor's duties upon transfer of a franchise and negotiate and judge the fee accordingly.

Most franchise agreements provide that the franchisor must approve the transfer of a franchise. The specific words used in the agreement regarding this point are critical and must be reviewed and negotiated carefully. If possible, a provision that requires that the franchisor will not "unreasonably withhold" consent to the transfer should be obtained. Franchisees should be very leery of any provision in the franchise agreement that allows the franchisor unfettered discretion in determining whether to allow a sale to be consummated or not.

Many franchise agreements provide that the franchisor has the right of first refusal to purchase a franchise. The concern here is that franchisees will be required to enter into an agreement with a prospective purchaser contingent upon the franchisor not exercising his/her right of first refusal. This may have a chilling effect on the sale since there are now contingencies over which the purchaser will not have control. Many potential franchise purchasers will not want to negotiate a full-scale agreement, only to be told that the franchisor has 30 or 60 or more days to determine whether or not it wants to buy the franchise property first.

If possible, the franchisee should negotiate a clause that provides that the franchisor has "a right of first offer." Under such an arrangement, the franchisee determines the price at which he/she will sell the franchise, then offers it back to the franchisor at that price and on specific terms acceptable to him/her. The franchisor would then have a specified time to determine whether or not to acquire the franchise, and, if not, the franchisee would be permitted to sell the franchise on the same terms to a third party without re-offering it to the franchisor.

Although it is best to have a right of first offer clause in the agreement from the inception of the franchise relationship, there is nothing to stop a franchisee from going to his/her franchisor, advising him/her of the intent to sell the franchise and asking the franchisor to waive the right of first refusal or revise the agreement to provide for a right of first offer. This is especially important if the franchisee proposes to transfer the franchise to a relative, or even to a trust set up for estate planning purposes.

> *Instead of letting the franchisor have "the first right of refusal" ask for a "right of first offer."*

Many franchise agreements provide for assignment by an individual franchisee to a corporation that the franchisee controls. Generally, there are small transfer fees involved in such a transaction. These fees should bear some relationship to the franchisor's actual (usually minimal) expense on such a transfer. Franchisees should also try to eliminate any clause requiring payment of a transfer fee when the transfer involves family members who have worked in the franchise.

A related issue arises when one of several partners or shareholders in a franchise seeks to sell their interest to partners or co–shareholders. In such instances, a franchise agreement may be as restrictive as it is when the franchise is being sold to an unrelated third party. Franchisees should seek to eliminate such restrictions, and the clause should be negotiated to provide that a transfer among franchisee partners or shareholders should be treated no differently than a transfer of a franchise from individual franchisees to corporate or partnership entities.

What the transferee gets is also important. Is the transferee required to execute the franchisor's new agreement or can he take an assignment of the existing agreement? From the transferee's perspective, this may be relevant for several reasons. These issues go to the heart of investment and equity. It is all about what franchisees can get for the time and money they have invested in the franchise. For example, if a franchisee is trying to sell a franchise two or three years into a 15-year term, it may be best for the transferee to assume the existing franchise agreement. If the franchise agreement is near the end of its term, or even halfway, the transferee may want to sign an agreement that is assumed, have the existing agreement extended or execute a new franchise agreement. The latter obviously raises several issues since a new franchise agreement will be substantially more beneficial to the franchisor than the one in existence since the inception of the franchise. Franchisees should try to obtain a provision that allows transferees to take assumption of the current franchise agreement. Another option is to include a provision in the franchise agreement stating that renewals, extensions or resale situations require the execution of a new franchise agreement on terms that are substantially similar to those contained in the original agreement.

Many franchise agreements require that, upon the sale of the franchise, the franchisee must sign a general release of any claims that he/she might have against the franchisor.

Many franchise agreements require that, upon the sale of the franchise, the franchisee must sign a general release of any claims that he/she might have against the franchisor. A franchisee should try to eliminate this provision. But a franchisee should try to negotiate with the franchisor and settle any differences prior to consummating the transfer transaction. If all else fails, try to obtain a release of claims from the franchisor as well as giving his or her release to the franchisor. This is called a mutual release of claims.

The issue of restrictive covenants is also a concern at the sale of a franchise. While it is not recognized within the lodging industry, restrictive covenants exist in many other industries. Most franchise agreements provide that, upon the termination of the franchise relationship for any reason, franchisees are restricted from engaging in a business competitive or similar to that of the franchisor. Franchisees should try to limit the applicability of or delete this provision entirely during the initial negotiations with the franchisor prior to purchasing the franchise.

Dispute Resolution

Generally speaking, there are three methods of dispute resolution that are available in various franchise agreements: mediation, arbitration and court proceedings.

Mediation of disputes allows the franchisor and the franchisee to present their positions relating to a dispute to an impartial third party who will then try to broker a settlement. Mediation is a valuable tool. However, there should not be a limitation on a franchisee's ability to proceed to court or to arbitration if the matter cannot be resolved quickly through mediation.

> *Franchisors and their lawyers have given this issue much thought and there are various reasons why they may choose one method over another.*

If mediation does not settle the dispute, or if mediation is not required by the franchise agreement, franchisees must decide whether they are compelled to arbitrate the dispute with the franchisor or whether they will go to court. Franchisors and their lawyers have given this issue much thought and there are various reasons why they may choose one method over another. Most likely, a franchise agreement will require arbitration of disputes because that method offers many advantages to the franchisor and many disadvantages to the franchisee. Although arbitration may be less expensive than going to court, franchisees should consider trying to avoid limiting their ability to go to court. If possible, a franchisee should negotiate mandatory arbitration provisions out of the franchise agreement.

Jury trials provide a better opportunity than arbitration to obtain redress for the wrongs a franchisor might have committed. Juries are made up of individuals who are more likely to have similar backgrounds and sensibilities to franchisees than arbitrators or mediators who are generally professionals and, sometimes exclusively, lawyers. Additionally, arbitration limits access to pre-trial or pre-hearing disclosure of information that may be essential to prove a case. Importantly, if a franchisee cannot go to court he/she cannot bring class action lawsuits, and in many states, he/she cannot receive punitive damages which a jury might award. That said, franchisees often have very little control over the method of dispute resolution, and if a franchisor has determined that arbitration is the way to go, it is unlikely that he/she will yield on the issue. Franchisees should, however, obtain as much flexibility within the process chosen by the franchisor as possible by utilizing the services of a franchisee attorney upfront, before signing the franchise agreement and buying the franchise.

Many franchise agreements provide that any arbitration will take place in the home state of the franchisor.

Many franchise agreements provide that any arbitration will take place in the home state of the franchisor. (Franchise agreements that do not provide for arbitration may also require that trials be held in the state where the franchisor is located.) Franchisees should, however, try to negotiate this provision and have the arbitration take place in the *franchisee's* home state. The franchisor, obviously, has substantially more resources and is better able to travel to different locations to conduct an arbitration, mediation or trial than most franchisees. To the extent possible, a franchisee should try to eliminate these clauses. Also, a franchisee should remember that in many states it is illegal for a franchisor to force the franchisee to give up the right to have a dispute arbitrated or brought to trial in *the franchisee's* home state. (A franchisee can check with his or her attorney to see if his or her state is one of those where venue for a dispute resides in the domicile of the franchisee.)

Even those franchise agreements that do not preclude access to court often restrict the rights of franchisees once they get there. For example, the agreement may limit a franchisee's right to a jury trial. Franchisees should try to eliminate this provision in negotiation. Many franchise agreements also provide that franchisees either cannot obtain punitive damages or they put a cap on punitive damages. Again, a franchisee should try to eliminate this provision. Similarly, some franchise agreements will limit damages for lost profits to one year, based solely on tax return information as opposed to full-scale operating information. Seek to eliminate such provisions whenever possible.

In many franchise agreements in which mediation or arbitration is mandated, the requirement is a one-way street. The franchisor will require franchisees to commence mediation or arbitration proceedings in the event they accuse their franchisor of breaching the agreement, but includes provisions permitting the franchisor to go to court under certain circumstances. Almost universally, a franchisor will permit itself the right to seek an injunction to stop a franchisee from violating trademarks. Franchisees should try to obtain a clause allowing them to obtain a court order prohibiting franchisors from violating the franchise agreement in certain ways, i.e., when encroachment occurs.

When the franchisee succeeds in litigation he/she should be permitted to seek reimbursement of attorneys' fees from the franchisor.

Frequently, franchise agreements provide that the cost of attorney's fees will be reimbursed to the franchisor in the event he/she is successful in pursuing claims against the franchisee or if the franchisee is unsuccessful in pursuing claims against the franchisor. At a minimum, franchisees should seek to have this clause modified to provide for mutuality. In the event that the franchisee succeeds in litigation he/she should be permitted to seek reimbursement of attorneys' fees from the franchisor. The provisions negotiated for this franchise should also be made clearly applicable when you either renew the franchise agreement or when you buy additional franchises.

A franchisee should delete provisions allowing the franchisor to buy the franchised business at below market price. Another provision showing up frequently in franchise agreements within the fast food industry is an option for the franchisor to purchase the franchisee's business at a below-market price. This is done in a variety of ways. In one, the franchisor gets to buy the main assets of the business so there is little left for the franchisee to sell at a fair price. In another, a price amount or formula is picked which will lead to a low-ball price, i.e. one-third of the prior year's sales instead of one-half. Sometimes, the agreement will say the franchisee gets nothing for the goodwill or going-concern value of the business. This means the franchisee ends up receiving liquidation value on the business.

Some agreements provide that the book value of the equipment and assets in the business should be the selling price, but that means the franchisee ends up with the value of worn equipment. Franchisees are entitled to fair market value for their businesses. Fair market value is typically a multiple of three to five times the adjusted cash flow received from the business. The low-ball price formulas in these options to purchase provisions allow the franchisor to take the real value of the business from the franchisee. Giving that power to the franchisor means he/she can use it later in order to persuade a franchisee to go along with something he/she does not want to do. Franchisees should not give franchisors a way to hurt them.

Confusion Over Marketing Assessment/Royalty Fees

Typically, franchisees are required to pay marketing assessment/royalty fees—usually ranging from one percent to sometimes more than five percent. Franchisees will need to carefully read and understand the paragraphs detailing the marketing assessment/royalty fees. Most confusion comes from franchisees agreeing to what was told to them by the franchise sales agent only to find different terms embedded in the agreement. Franchisees are misled by franchisors when they are informed for example that 1.3 percent of a hotelier's gross room revenue will be charged for the marketing assessment fees. However, the agreement may also read:

"In addition to the 1.3% the franchisee agrees to pay monthly commencing with the commencement date, a supplemental marketing fee, equal to 28 cents per day times the specific room count."

This can equal more than three percent in marketing assessment fees for an average 60-unit hotel. In this example the franchisee advisory council made up of existing franchisees voted and approved the increase of the 28 cents per day per room cost. However, the new first-time franchisee is unaware of and is not informed of the additional 28 cents per day per room cost until after the initial franchise fees are paid and the agreement is ready to be signed. At that point there is no negotiating.

Consequently, it is very important that franchisees understand what is agreed upon and actually read for themselves the agreement that is drawn up for their signature. A good place to look is in the back of the Uniform Franchise Offering Circular (UFOC). A copy of the agreement is attached as part of the UFOC. A franchisee should have this clarified before the initial franchise fees are paid. The franchisor may not be willing to negotiate after they have the franchisee's money.

The General Release and Covenant Not To Sue The Franchisor

Another provision showing up in many franchise agreements are covenants not to sue the franchisor. This covenant waives the franchisee's rights, as well as his/her respective representatives, successors and heirs etc., not to sue the franchisor whether the fault be known or unknown. The *not to sue* covenant survives through the termination of the license. This covenant is often not reciprocal. It does not stop the franchisor from suing the franchisee for any known or unknown reasons.

This covenant waives the franchisee's rights, as well as his/her respective representatives, successors and heirs etc., not to sue the franchisor whether the fault be known or unknown.

Here is a typical example of this covenant:

General Release and Covenant Not to Sue. Licensee and its respective heirs, representatives, successors and assigns, hereby release, remise and forever discharge Licensor and its parent, subsidiaries and affiliates and their directors, employees, agents, successors and assigns from any and all claims, whether known or unknown, of any kind or nature, absolute or contingent, if any there be, at law or in equity from the beginning of time up to, and including the date of Licensor's execution of this License, and Licensee and its respective heirs, representatives, successors and assigns do hereby covenant and agree that they will not institute any suit or action at law or otherwise against Licensor, directly or indirectly relating to any claim released hereby by Licensee. This release and covenant not to sue shall survive the termination of this License. Licensee shall take whatever steps are necessary or appropriate to carry out the terms of this release and covenant not to sue upon Licensor's request.

A franchisee must review the agreement and search for this type of covenant. Again, a good place to search is the UFOC. A franchisee should ask the franchisor executive what he or she thinks about this covenant and should see if they understand fairness verses unfairness. A franchisor should demand that it be deleted from the agreement. At the very least it must be mutually applicable for both franchisor and franchisee alike.

CHAPTER II
NEW MILLENIUM ENCROACHMENT

Among the numerous considerations in choosing a site for a new franchise, there are several critical factors a prospective franchisee should evaluate. There is a definite correlation between the location, the number of customers that frequent the area and the profitability of success or failure of the new business.

Ideally, a prospective franchise buyer should consider retaining an independent consultant knowledgeable in the relevant industry and market area to research the suitability of the proposed location. These consultants provide feasibility studies that analyze the demographics, traffic patterns, routes of ingress and egress, existence of competing brands in the same market and ownership of adjacent (occupied or vacant) properties.

It is only prudent that prospective investors spend the money it costs for these studies, often several thousand dollars. When one considers the emotional and capital investments made on a franchise project, not conducting a feasibility study is "penny wise and pound foolish." A feasibility study might just reveal that the project is not worthwhile in the particular location chosen by the investor.

Franchise investors should also seek information as to the franchisor's plans for expansion and development.

Franchise investors should also seek information as to the franchisor's plans for expansion and development, in other words, whether the company plans to add similar properties in the area, develop as-yet uncharted territory, add a competing brand owned by the same company or pursue another channel of distribution. Where possible, the franchisee should seek confirmation in writing from the franchisor as to the existence or lack of existence of such plans.

What is Encroachment?

Challenges to a franchisor's encroachment—also called cannibalization—arise most frequently when a franchisor places a new business within such close proximity to an existing franchise that it jeopardizes the existing franchise's continued success. The new business will likely have a negative impact on sales and divert consumer traffic. The franchisor's placement of a competing site can have a substantial effect on profits, particularly when the competition is company-owned.

When is Enough Enough?

A second, more subtle form of encroachment best illustrated within the fast food industry results when a franchisor institutes alternative channels of distribution that the franchisee neither knew of nor expected at the time of signing the contract. These include the franchisor's expansion via use of kiosks, mail order, Internet sales, grocery store sales, etc.

Franchisors frequently maintain that the franchise system derives overall benefit from the expanding market share and increased brand recognition ("legitimate business considerations"). This point of view overlooks the franchisee's justifiable expectations of success in the market and his or her enduring obligation to pay royalties and other fees during the entire contract period—regardless of any financial decline resulting from a competing franchise. Of course, the franchisor will receive royalties and fees from each of its franchisees, and thus, has ample incentive to saturate the market. Franchisors receive increased revenue when sales increase, even if those sales are at the expense of individual franchisees' profits. Franchisees, by contrast, must maintain quality standards and pay marketing assessment fees/royalties whether or not their franchise is profitable.

Self-Defense Against Encroachment

Franchisees can reduce the risk of becoming a victim of unreasonable encroachment in a variety of ways. The best place to begin is, of course, at the beginning. Before buying a franchise, a potential franchisee should seek the advice of experienced franchisee counsel to help balance the scales and to seek to implement contractual safeguards against any prospective overreaching of the franchisor.

> *The franchisee and his/her advisors should evaluate the nature of the existing competition surrounding the proposed location.*

The franchisee and his/her advisors should evaluate the nature of the existing competition surrounding the proposed location. The franchisor's UFOC will offer limited help regarding any "protected territory" for the franchisee. The UFOC will probably offer limited information in the way of the franchisor's criteria and policies and procedures for site selection.

> *Ask the franchisor to waive the right to develop other, competing businesses or franchise systems using the same or different proprietary marks.*

Counsel should make every effort to reconcile the encroachment issue at the time of contracting to ensure that the franchisee will know what to expect. Ideally, the franchisor would grant the franchisee an exclusive territory, agree not to use alternative channels to distribute its products and waive the right to develop other, competing businesses or franchise systems using the same or different proprietary marks. This latter provision will protect the franchisee in the event the franchisor merges with or acquires a competitor and attempts to operate both systems simultaneously.

Since the definition of encroachment typically calls for a situation-specific factual analysis, it is impossible to define absolute boundaries that would be applicable to every case, i.e. three miles. However, the contract should address the franchisee's expectations and expressly reserve the right to damages in the event of the franchisor's cannibalization on the existing franchisee's business.

Most major franchisors will not agree to include provisions which would significantly reduce their freedom to develop other locations or to use other distribution methods. However, some franchisors now include procedures in their contracts for addressing encroachment. While these provisions seldom provide complete protection against unreasonable encroachment, they may limit the franchisor's freedom, or provide a claim in the event the franchisor fails to comply with his/her own procedures.

If the franchisor persists in refusing to negotiate the contract terms and the franchisee is still determined to join that franchise system, he/she should be fully aware of the risks and potential for encroachment. But he/she should also be on the lookout for other tools to employ to limit unreasonable encroachment.

Franchise Agreements vs. the Sales Pitch

Or, Be Wary of the Merger and Integration Clause.

The "merger and integration clause," a seemingly innocuous paragraph often buried at the very end of the franchise contract, often works to obliterate the oral promises that the franchisor may have made prior to contracting. For example, the salesperson's verbal comments may involve the franchisee's interest in obtaining a protected or exclusive territory. The franchisee must get all important representations that he/she is relying upon included in writing in the franchise contract documents. If they are not written in the contract documents, the merger and integration clause will limit, and often eliminate, the franchisee's ability to hold the franchisor to those oral promises—even if the franchisee relied on them in deciding to buy into the concept.

Keep Your Ears Open

Even franchisors who refuse to commit in their contract to protect franchisees against encroachment may have occasion to reassure franchisees that they won't unreasonably encroach. Depending upon the circumstances, those franchisors may be prevented from acting contrary to those assurances. Such statements, if made after the contract is signed, may be enforced by courts in some jurisdictions as oral modifications to the franchise contract. Other courts use legal theories such as "estoppel" to prevent a franchisor from acting in a manner contrary to its statements and conduct. Franchisees should pay close attention to such statements when made, and document them to the extent possible. As always, obtaining the commitments in writing is the best protection a franchisee has.

Franchise Statutes

In addition to remedies for breach of contract, franchisees in certain states have the benefit of protective legislation governing the sale and operation of franchise systems. Notably, the extent and nature of regulation differs substantially from one jurisdiction to another, and prospective franchisees should consult an attorney regarding a particular state's law prior to consummating the franchise sales transaction.

Legislation specifically regulating encroachment of existing franchisees is a recent, and thus far limited, phenomenon.

Legislation specifically regulating encroachment of existing franchisees is a recent, and thus far limited, phenomenon. The most notable legislation on this topic is the Iowa Franchise Investment Act ("Iowa law"). Under the Iowa law:

> If a franchisor develops or grants to a franchisee the right to develop a new property or location which sells essentially the same goods or services under the same trademark, service mark, trade name, logotype, or other commercial symbol as an existing franchisee and the new outlet or location has an adverse effect on the gross sales of the existing franchisee's outlet or location, the existing adversely affected franchisee has a cause of action for monetary damages in an amount calculated pursuant to section 3, unless [certain enumerated conditions] apply.

There are exceptions to the statute of limitations on its use, and it is under frequent legislative attack. Franchisees interested in protecting their businesses against encroachment should pay close attention to the Iowa legislation and to opportunities for passage of similar legislation in their states.

Franchise regulatory statutes may be a source of indirect remedies for encroachment, even if the statutes do not address encroachment directly. Many franchise statutes provide a claim for a franchisor's misrepresentation or concealment of material facts in connection with the sale of a franchise or for acting in "bad faith" after it is sold and the franchised business has been established. These laws, where available, may provide a remedy for broken promises not to encroach or concealment of material information regarding encroachment policies, practices or plans.

Judicial Decisions on Encroachment

The most important and most controversial legal theory that courts use to limit franchisor encroachment is the implied covenant of good faith and fair dealing.

Even if the franchisor did not agree to avoid unreasonable encroachment, the law may limit the franchisor's ability to encroach. The most important and most controversial legal theory that courts use to limit franchisor encroachment is the implied covenant of good faith and fair dealing. Interpreted according to state law, the implied covenant recognizes standards of conduct not explicitly stated in the franchise agreement by implying into the franchise contract an obligation to deal with the franchisee in good faith and in a commercially reasonable manner. Franchisee advocates view the doctrine as essential in preserving the franchisee's justifiable expectations of its relationship with the franchisor. But the courts have been very slow and reluctant to use it to protect franchisees.

Generally, this claim focuses on contractual provisions which give the franchisor broad unilateral discretion. Franchisees typically allege that the franchisor has exercised its power arbitrarily, capriciously or inconsistently with the parties' reasonable expectations.

Policy? What Policy?

Franchisors often have policies and procedures relating to site selection, which often include encroachment issues, i.e., the franchisor's in-house impact policies. While franchise contracts seldom require the franchisor to follow such policies, franchisors typically do so. When the policies are not followed, affected franchisees may have a claim based upon the franchisor's failure to follow its own policies. Some franchise agreements do not include any territorial issues and therefore the parties rely on the system's in-house impact policies. One problem with that—policies can and do change at the sole discretion of the franchisor. This means a three mile protected territory can become one mile through the unilateral and arbitrary decision of the franchisor. And some states restrict the enforcement of policy issues not spelled out in the franchise agreement, arguing that the franchise agreement has a superior right over any policies.

New Age Encroachment: C-Stores, Supermarkets and the Internet

In recent years, many franchisors have focused their distribution efforts on getting their product to consumers wherever they can find them.

In fast food franchised industries, the implied covenant has also been applied, along with legal theories, to limit a franchisor's ability to sell branded products through alternative channels. In recent years, many franchisors have focused their distribution efforts on getting their product to consumers wherever they can find them. Franchisors who traditionally sold branded products only through franchised stores suddenly developed an interest in selling their products in supermarkets, kiosks, convenience stores, movie theaters, over the Internet, through catalogues and elsewhere. This led to a subtle, but very devastating, form of encroachment. Franchisees with free-standing traditional outlets might experience sales declines but could not point to the comparatively obvious culprit of a new outlet just like theirs standing a few blocks away. The franchisee, whose investments in facilities and advertising over many years had created an awareness of and market for the franchisor's branded products in that area suddenly found the fruits of their labor being siphoned off by these *alternative channel* distribution strategies.

Courts and franchisees alike have struggled to define what level of protection is available to the franchisee when the encroachment comes from the use of alternative channels of distribution. However, several courts have employed the implied covenant and other theories to hold that there are limits on franchisors' ability to distribute its products through alternative channels when franchisees are harmed by that distribution. Recently, a federal district court held that a franchisor whose contract expressly stated that the franchisor reserved the right to distribute its products in alternative channels, including supermarkets, might still violate the implied covenant of good faith and fair dealing by doing just that.

Franchisees often enter into franchise relation-ships before either they or their franchisor has even thought about alternative channels of distribution.

Franchisees faced with *new age* encroachment from alternative channels of distribution should not assume they have no rights or remedies simply because their contract provides none. Franchisees often enter into franchise relationships before either they or their franchisor has even thought about alternative channels of distribution. As a result, many franchisees may have received and relied upon franchisor communications that suggested that the franchisor would not engage in any other method of distribution. The UFOC is supposed to disclose this but frequently fails to do so. Just because the encroachment isn't coming from next door doesn't mean there's nothing to be done about it. The law is just beginning to develop in this area. Franchisees need to know, however, what their franchisor intends to do concerning alternative channels of distribution. Again, the UFOC is supposed to disclose this. Franchisees should ask their franchisors about their intentions regarding alternative channel development and endeavor to get them to state, on the record, those intentions. If the franchisor intends to use alternative channels of development, the franchisee should ask what role franchisees will have in such projects and how the franchisor intends to avoid encroachment problems. And, it doesn't hurt to ask again down the road. Franchisors often change their policies and their programs without consulting or even advising their own franchisees.

Alternative channels of distribution is a form of encroachment that typically affects large numbers of franchisees simultaneously.

Alternative channels of distribution is a form of encroachment that typically affects large numbers of franchisees simultaneously. The best solution to this sort of encroachment may, therefore, be to negotiate as a group, through an independent franchisee association or otherwise, with the franchisor. Franchisees may be able to negotiate limits on what types of distribution the franchisor can undertake and ways to reduce the impact of alternative channel distribution on existing franchisees; or the opportunity for existing franchisees to participate in or receive some of the benefits from alternative channel development.

The law of encroachment is still developing in many jurisdictions. As a result, it is often difficult to predict how the courts will decide encroachment disputes, particularly where they involve franchise agreements whose territorial clauses are either ambiguous or missing all together. A franchisee's best protection is always clear and precise contractual language as to the parties' respective rights and expectations. Most important, however, is to be vigilant of terms that could allow the franchisor the unbridled discretion to place a new franchise next door, or down the road on the next exit.

Franchisees almost always gain leverage and greater rights with respect to their franchisors by organizing and presenting their requests as a group and by retaining competent and experienced franchisee lawyers to assist them in obtaining and enforcing their contract and other legal rights. When faced with an encroachment problem, a franchisee should review carefully his entire franchise history, including documents and relevant oral communications, with experienced franchise litigation counsel. This is true even if the franchise contract doesn't prohibit encroachment.

CHAPTER III
WHY THE FRANCHISOR WANTS TO STAY OUT OF COURT

Introduction to Alternative Dispute Resolution (ADR)

In almost every franchise agreement, the franchisor has deliberately chosen the battlefield on which it will engage its franchisees in all future disputes. As with every other provision contained in the franchise agreement, the selection of the particular battlefield is made solely to enhance the probability that the franchisor, not the franchisee, will be victorious. A franchisee should not underestimate the significance of the battlefield analogy. When rules of engagement are implemented, it will be total, all-out war in which the franchisee may sustain fatal injuries. This chapter, addressing the good, the bad and the ugly of Alternative Dispute Resolution "ADR," explains why franchisors choose particular battlefields of engagement, details the advantages and disadvantages inherent in each strategy and advises franchisees on how to counterattack to foil the enemy. Each field of engagement has potential good and bad aspects, but each battlefield has one thing in common—an ugly experience awaiting its combatants. Even franchisees not currently at war with franchisors must realize that it is incumbent upon them to understand the rules of engagement prior to any declaration of war.

Franchisors like to tout the advantages of "alternative dispute resolution" or "ADR." This chapter explains why that is and why ADR may not be such a good idea for franchisees.

Traditional Litigation in Our Judicial System

Many franchisors have determined that the traditional judicial system, in which disputes arising from the franchise agreement are resolved in a court of law represent a horror to be avoided at all costs. Trials may lead to runaway juries, franchisors believe, where sympathy for the franchisee may lead to huge verdicts and awards of multiple damages and/or punitive damages and attorneys fees that threaten the existence of the franchise system. Thus, before we proceed to a discussion of dispute resolution alternatives, we must begin with an analysis of why franchisors seek to avoid the traditional courtroom setting.

What Franchisors Say About Why the Courtroom Should Be Avoided

There are very sound reasons for any litigant wanting to avoid litigation in the traditional courtroom setting.

There are very sound reasons for any litigant wanting to avoid litigation in the traditional courtroom setting. Typically, the franchisor will focus on the following reasons when explaining the need to consider ADR:

Time: Traditional litigation in light of today's congested courtroom dockets is too time consuming. It may take years to obtain the resolution of a franchise dispute. Courts are far too busy with criminal trials to provide civil litigants an opportunity to be heard.

Expense: Traditional litigation, with full discovery, dispositive motions, legal memoranda and lengthy trials, is far too expensive a method to resolve franchise disputes.

Burden: Traditional litigation, with its full complement of discovery (production of documents, interrogatories, depositions, etc.), is too burdensome on the parties and only adds to the excessive length and expense of litigation.

Finality: Litigation can go on forever without resolution, due to the availability of seemingly endless appeals.

Each of these factors contains a certain degree of truth. Civil litigation can be extremely time consuming, lengthy, burdensome on the parties and, at times, apparently never-ending.

Franchisors typically seek to outspend the franchisee in litigation fees and expenses by two to fivefold in an attempt to exhaust the franchisee's ability to continue the litigation.

However, these are not the real reasons a franchisor chooses ADR over traditional litigation. The franchisor is not overly concerned about any of these points. First, time is not an important factor when the franchisor is the defendant. It is typical strategy for a defendant-franchisor to extend the time period for discovery, dispositive motions and trial in an attempt to exhaust the franchisee's resources and determination. Second, the franchisor often uses the significant imbalance in financial resources to force the franchisee into submission. Franchisors will typically seek to outspend the franchisee in litigation fees and expenses by two to five fold in an attempt to exhaust the franchisee's ability to continue the litigation. Third, the burden of litigation on the franchisee is usually much greater than the burden on the franchisor. The franchisor, after forcing the franchisee to produce every scrap of paper in his/her possession, often stonewalls his/her own discovery production, producing reams of worthless paper but little if anything of value, unless ordered to do so by the court. Fourth, the defendant-franchisor is not interested in finality; rather, he/she will seek to out last the franchisee, often filing counterclaims for past-due royalties or advertising fund contributions or termination, hoping that the franchisee will be forced to give up the fight before the final result is obtained. There is a method to this madness; the large majority of cases settle prior to trial, often with results far more favorable to the franchisor than the franchisee.

What the Franchisor Really Means When He/She Says the Courtroom Should Be Avoided

Therefore, when the franchisor says he/she wants to avoid traditional courtroom litigation, we need to examine what that really means:

Time: Given enough time, the franchisee might prove its case against the franchisor. The franchisor must believe there is a better system where he/she has greater control over the rules of engagement and greater chance for ultimate victory. ADR is faster because it restricts the ability of the franchisee to conduct discovery, shortens the time period for hearings and retracts access to franchisor personnel.

Expense: The franchisor is more concerned with winning than with expense. In fact, ADR may actually be more costly with its expensive filing, administrative and arbitrator/mediator fees. The franchisor wants to spend its money where it has the greatest chances for success.

Burden: The franchisor does not want to engage in discovery where it may be ordered to produce its internal records and documents and subject its management people to depositions. Consider the lengths to which the Clinton White House went to preclude producing documents or witnesses to the independent counsel, to better understand the reluctance of the franchisor to allow a franchisee unfettered access to its records. Discovery is more limited under ADR than in traditional litigation.

Finality: When the franchisor is successful, finality is important. Under ADR, there are no appeals. And if the franchisee is successful, the franchisor still benefits by producing no precedent-setting value in the decision. Thus, other franchisees cannot take advantage of the decision against the franchisor.

A franchisor chooses that battlefield where it believes the franchisor will receive a fair hearing on the merits of its claims.

What this all comes down to is the element of control. A franchisor chooses that battlefield where he/she believes he/she has the greatest power to have a fair hearing on the merits of his/her claims. The primary reason a franchisor seeks to avoid traditional litigation is because the franchisor does not have sufficient control over the decision. Thus ADR, whether it be mediation or arbitration, has become an attractive resolution vehicle for franchisors because they believe it provides them greater control over the decision-makers, the process and the ultimate result.

What Traditional Litigation Provides the Franchisee

For franchisees, even with the realities of time, expense, burdens of discovery, and complexities of court procedural and substantive practice, traditional litigation holds certain advantages over ADR in franchise disputes. As this chapter's focus is on ADR, some of the advantages and disadvantages of litigation are highlighted here for purposes of comparison with ADR.

Advantages and Disadvantages of Traditional Litigation: A Franchisee Perspective

ADVANTAGES OF TRIALS	DISADVANTAGES OF TRIALS
Right to full discovery	Expense and burden of Discovery.
Injunctive relief status quo pending trial; ex: no termination.	May involve discovery and evidentiary hearing. Risk of Bond requirement
Trial before judge or jury.	Time delays—may take years.
Multiple/punitive damages and attorney fees.	Multiple/punitive damages and attorney fees against franchisee.
Right to appeal.	Endless process; franchisee can lose victory.
Res judicata precedent.	No good if not in business.
Public forum.	Public knows franchisee's business.

Overview of Arbitration Proceeding

Many franchise agreements now provide that all disputes between the franchisor and franchisee arising out of the franchise relationship shall be resolved in a binding arbitration proceeding. Typically, the franchise agreement provides that the arbitration proceeding shall be conducted in the franchisor's home state under the law of the franchisor's state. The franchisor has chosen to engage the franchisee in an arbitration proceeding because it believes this battlefield offers the franchisor a greater chance of victory while limiting the impact any losses may have on the franchisor in its dealing with other franchisees.

In one major franchise arbitration proceeding, the franchisee had to pay AAA filing fees of more than $30,000.

The arbitration clause eliminates the right of the franchisee (except in very limited circumstances) to have the dispute heard in a court of law. This means not only that there will be no jury trial, but that other rights associated with the court system are also gone, including: full discovery, rules of evidence, rules of procedure, full trial, the right to appeal and a public forum. Also, the administrative cost of the legal system changes dramatically, as arbitration has much higher filing fees, administrative costs and fees for the arbitrator's services. Filing fees at the American Arbitration Association (AAA) are based on a percentage of the damages sought in the arbitration demand. In addition, the arbitrator is paid at an hourly rate for his or her services. These fees are borne by both parties. In one major franchise arbitration proceeding, the franchisee had to pay AAA filing fees of more than $30,000.00.

While brevity may have its advantages, such a shortened arbitration proceeding may deprive the franchisee a fair opportunity.

Also, after franchisees have paid all this money for the arbitration proceeding, they may receive far less for their money than they do in court. Arbitration proceedings differ substantially from the traditional litigation. Not only is discovery curtailed dramatically in arbitration, the hearing itself is often greatly reduced in comparison to the length of a trial. For instance, in one arbitration proceeding, the parties were limited to eight hours to put on their case plus four hours for their respective damage experts. Thus, the arbitration proceeding was conducted in just three days, whereas a trial in the same matter may have taken three weeks or longer. While brevity may have its advantages, such a shortened arbitration proceeding may deprive the franchisee a fair opportunity to be heard. Then, once the arbitrator makes his decision, there is usually a one paragraph statement made announcing the victorious party and the amount of damages (if any). The case is then over. There is no right of appeal. If a franchisee gets a *bad* decision, there is no avenue to have it reviewed, even if the arbitrator is dead wrong on the law.

Many people believe that the advantages of arbitration overcome its shortfalls, providing the parties a less expensive, much faster method to obtain a just resolution of franchise disputes. The franchisor obviously believes that he/she has greater control over the outcome of an arbitration proceeding, with a direct role in choosing the arbitrator and defining the rules of engagement, than in a trial in which the judge has the ultimate control.

Overview of Mediation Proceeding

In the past several years, many franchisors have modified their franchise agreements to include a provision requiring most franchise disputes to seek resolution through a mandatory, though non-binding, mediation process. In mediation, an independent mediator serves as facilitator to assist the parties in obtaining an agreed-upon resolution to the issue under dispute. The mediator has no authority to issue any decision. There is only a resolution if the parties enter into an agreement on how to settle the action. The mediation proceeding is designed to be a process whereby two parties, each of whom is committed to reach a resolution of the dispute, can come together quickly, in a confidential proceeding, to negotiate a settlement of the problem. Obviously, it only works if both of the parties truly desire to reach a fair business resolution or compromise that both sides can live with.

When the mediator is successful, the parties are able to reach a resolution.

The role of the mediator is to engage the parties in discussion to reach an accord. Part of his/her role will be maintaining open communication between the parties, offering different resolution options and trying to point the parties to common ground. To be successful, a mediator needs to have the legal and business expertise to evaluate the respective positions of the parties, pointing out the strengths and weaknesses of each, and the strength to lead the parties to a resolution that can work for both sides. When the mediator is successful, the parties are able to reach resolution, beyond the scope of purely legalistic remedy, that will avoid an expensive, protracted, all-out war.

That said, mediation may not be appropriate for every type of dispute. It may be an attractive vehicle for a franchise dispute where the parties will continue to have an ongoing relationship following the resolution of the dispute. However, it is probably not an attractive option when the issues in dispute challenge the very core of the franchise system, though even in this circumstance there have been exceptions.

Mediation gives franchisors the power to "just say no!"

The franchisor has a strong sense of control in the mediation process, with a significant role in the selection of the mediator. Franchisors usually designate particular mediation services that will be utilized for the process, also giving them additional input in the rules of engagement. Finally, mediation gives franchisors the power to "just say no!" at any time and bring the process to a rapid, screeching conclusion. The mediator cannot force a resolution upon the franchisor. The franchisor thus retains the ultimate weapon—the ability to withdraw from the proceeding and choose or force the franchisee onto another battlefield.

The mediation process also often has the effect of forcing the franchisee to disclose his/her claims and his/her strategy long before he/she can file a claim in court or even in arbitration. This can only hurt the franchisee down the road, especially if the franchisor stonewalls the mediation and it fails to produce a negotiated settlement. The pyramid chart here depicts how the franchisor's control changes within each category.

CONTROLLING
INTERESTS

FRANCHISOR'S ABILITY
TO CONTROL

I. MEDIATION
Mediator has no authority to bind parties.
No discovery; no appeals; no punitive damages.
Franchisor most able to control outcome of dispute.

II. ARBITRATION
Arbitrator has authority to issue binding decision.
Limited discovery; limited precedent value; almost no appeals.
Arbitrators potentially biased toward franchisor-area of expertise.
Franchisor has some control over arbitrator; discovery; hearing and remedies.

III. LITIGATION
Litigation offers full enforcement—judge, appeals, precedent.
The Full Monty of discovery—documents; depositions and interrogatories.
Public evidentiary hearing in a courtroom: full trial by jury; full appellate rights.
Franchisor has least ability to control the ultimate outcome and resolution of litigation.

The Franchisor's Perceived Ability To Control the Proceeding Ultimately Determines the Selection of the Battlefield

The primary focus of the franchisor, in determining whether to include in his/her franchise agreement a provision requiring mediation, arbitration or traditional trial litigation for resolution of disputes with his/her franchisees, is selecting that battlefield on which it has the greatest control over the ultimate outcome and the franchisee has the least opportunity to make his/her case on the merits. The franchisor progression away from litigation to arbitration, mediation or other ADR alternatives charts a course of franchisor control.

ARBITRATION ADVANTAGES AND DISADVANTAGES

The key differences between an arbitration and a lawsuit are who decides the case and the forum in which the case is decided.

Who Decides the Case

> *Arbitrators will also typically have more business experience than the typical juror and may be able to understand business problems better than a juror.*

Arbitrators are usually either businesspeople or lawyers. It is rare to find either on a jury. This difference can be either an advantage or a disadvantage, depending on the case. Arbitrators will usually be more familiar with franchise agreements and other contracts than typical jurors. Arbitrators will also typically have more business experience than the typical juror and may be able to understand business problems better than a juror.

On the other hand, the arbitrators are not likely to have as much natural sympathy for *little David* trying to take on the franchisor *Goliath*. Thus, they will not be as likely to punish the franchisor with punitive damages as will a sympathetic jury.

Forum for Deciding the Case

Lawsuits are conducted under fairly strict rules of procedure, evidence and substantive law. Decisions are made by trained judges who, at least in theory, are required to follow the rules without regard to personal feelings or beliefs.

Arbitration is conducted under more relaxed rules, typically those of the American Arbitration Association (AAA). The arbitration rules are generally designed to streamline procedures and to obtain a result with less expenditure of time and money than a lawsuit. As a result, there is usually much less pretrial discovery and motion practice in an arbitration. This can be beneficial to the franchisee unless he/she needs to obtain a large amount of material or testimony from the franchisor or its employees. When that is necessary, the informal nature of the rules becomes a disadvantage to the franchisee.

There are several other important disadvantages to franchisees in the arbitration procedure. Since franchise agreements usually require arbitration to be conducted at the home office of the franchisor, franchisees have the additional expense and inconvenience of having to go to a distant location.

There is typically no subpoena power to compel witnesses to attend an arbitration.

There is typically no subpoena power to compel witnesses to attend an arbitration. This means franchisees must count on the generosity of those needed as witnesses to go wherever the arbitration is being held.

Another disadvantage in arbitration procedures is that class actions are prohibited and franchisees may be precluded from obtaining system-wide relief from the franchisor's onerous activities or contract provisions. Franchisees may also be precluded from obtaining punitive damages, depending on which state law applies.

The franchisee does have an advantage, however, in a case for which the arbitrators may give equitable relief. Since arbitrators do not always follow the law quite as closely as a judge, there is a possibility for relief in situations in which franchisees have been wronged, but could not recover in court because of some legal technicality or contract language drawn up by the franchisor.

For example, many courts simply refuse to permit the franchisee to get any benefit from the implied covenant of good faith and fair dealing, which is supposed to apply to all contracts. Using so-called *equitable* principals, the arbitrators may give the franchisee relief from encroachment, punitive inspections, product purchase requirements and other detrimental franchisor actions when a lawsuit would fail. Courts invariably confirm arbitration awards unless there is clear evidence of fraud or other irregularity, even if the judge might decide the case differently.

WAYS TO AVOID ARBITRATION

Should a franchisee determine that it is in his/her best interest to have a dispute with the franchisor decided by a lawsuit rather than by arbitration, the franchisee will need to find a way around the arbitration provision in the franchise agreement. While there are some legal arguments which can help avoid arbitration, there are only a few of these and the courts like to require arbitration whenever possible.

> *Some arbitration clauses refer all disputes between franchisee and franchisor to arbitration, while others only call for arbitration of disputes arising out of the agreement.*

Scope of the Arbitration

The first thing to look at is the scope of the arbitration provision itself. Typically, courts enforce arbitration clauses as they are written. Although franchisors all tend to use the same forms in their franchise agreements, they are not completely uniform. Some arbitration clauses refer *all disputes* between franchisee and franchisor to arbitration, while others only call for arbitration of *disputes arising out of this agreement*. In this case, disputes not arising directly out of the franchise agreement are not automatically subject to arbitration.

Which Law Applies

Most franchise disputes involve interstate commerce so federal law usually applies and federal law is very favorable to arbitration.

Courts deciding whether to apply an arbitration clause to a particular dispute look to federal law if the dispute involves interstate commerce. Most franchise disputes involve interstate commerce so federal law usually applies and federal law is very favorable to arbitration. However, if the dispute does not involve interstate commerce, state law will apply. Many states have adopted the Uniform Arbitration Act, which is also favorable to arbitration. Other states have different statutes and case law. Some, such as Alabama, actually prohibit enforcement of arbitration clauses. If the Federal Arbitration Act applies, however, it will override a contrary state statute.

Fraud in Inducement to Enter Arbitration Agreement

One argument for excluding disputes from arbitration is that the franchisee was induced by the franchisor's fraud to enter into the arbitration clause. This is a very difficult argument to win because franchisees must distinguish between fraud involving the entire franchise agreement and fraud involving only the arbitration clause. For example, if the franchisee claims the franchisor lied in its earnings claims or lied about how much help the franchisor would give to get franchisee to sign the agreement, those disputes will go to arbitration. To avoid arbitration with this fraud argument a franchisee must show there was separate fraud by the franchisor which induced the franchisee to enter into the arbitration clause itself, as opposed to the entire contract. Such a situation might arise if the franchisor promised, before the franchisee signed the agreement, that the arbitration clause would not be enforced.

Existence, Illegality or Unconscionability of Contract

If there is a question about the existence of the agreement containing the arbitration clause—such as whether a signature was forged or whether the franchisor altered the agreement without the franchisee's knowledge and consent after it was signed—this issue will be decided by a court. Courts will also decide claims that a contract is illegal, unconscionable or otherwise unenforceable. However, if the claimed illegality goes to only a portion of the contract, the dispute is arbitrable.

Unequal Application of the Arbitration Clause

> *Some franchise agreements require the franchisee to arbitrate any claim it may have against the franchisor while allowing the franchisor go to court for most or all of its claims against the franchisee.*

Some franchise agreements require the franchisee to arbitrate any claim it may have against the franchisor while allowing the franchisor go to court for most or all of its claims against the franchisee. Courts are finding such unevenly applied arbitration clauses unconscionable and unenforceable.

Statute of Limitations

In some jurisdictions, including the federal courts of appeal for the third, sixth, seventh, tenth and eleventh circuits, the courts determine the applicability of the statutes of limitation. In other jurisdictions, including the second, fourth, fifth, eighth, ninth and District of Columbia circuits, that issue is left to the arbitrators.

Waiver of Right to Arbitrate

Courts have held that a party may waive his/her right to arbitrate by engaging in conduct such as filing and prosecuting a lawsuit, which tends to renounce the right to enforce an arbitration clause on the other party.

Reorganization or Bankruptcy

It may be possible to avoid arbitration by filing for reorganization or bankruptcy and rescinding the entire franchise agreement, although this is not a certainty.

MEDIATION: ADVANTAGES AND DISADVANTAGES OF THE MEDIATION PROCESS TO RESOLVE A FRANCHISE DISPUTE

The Advantages of Using Mediation to Resolve Franchise Disputes

One commentator describes the advantages of the mediation process by reciting the *Four C's:* (1) Confidential, (2) Control, (3) Cost effective and (4) Cwick (Old English for Quick). Collaboration could be included as a fifth "C," because, as already noted, there is no resolution unless the parties collaborate to reach consensus or fair resolution. Putting the Five C's together brings about the following description of the mediation process:

A process where disagreeing parties come together in a confidential, controlled environment for discussion under the direction of the mediator, generally in a one-day, cost-effective session, to collaborate in effort to reach a resolution. While the mediator controls the direction of the discussion, the parties control whether the process achieves ultimate resolution of the dispute at issue.

Mediation Provides an Avenue for Rapid Resolution

Mediation seeks to bring parties together as quickly as possible.

A major attraction to mediation is that it provides an avenue for quick resolution of a franchise dispute. Mediation seeks to bring parties together as quickly as possible. The mediation provision of a franchise agreement typically provides that mediation shall begin by one party filing a written request upon the other to mediate an existing dispute. There is also a mechanism for selection of a mediator. Mediators are often retired judges or experienced attorneys or businesspeople with expertise in the particular specialty area. After the mediator is selected, the parties are asked to submit *position papers* which outline the factual circumstances, the pertinent franchise documents, the issue in dispute, the law supporting the respective parties' positions and the relief sought through the mediation process. The mediator will then schedule the mediation session and outline any rules that will govern the procedure. Such rules often require that each party be represented by a person with decision-making authority (i.e., the power to bind that party to an agreement).

Generally, the mediation session begins with opening statements. The mediator will then direct the proceedings; sometimes meeting with the parties together and, at other times, meeting with the parties separately. The focus of these meetings will be to narrow the issues in dispute, identify the proposals for resolution, consider the alternative of protracted litigation in the event the parties are unable to resolve the dispute, evaluate for each side the strengths and weaknesses of the respective factual and legal positions and seek to guide the parties to resolution of the dispute. The resolution will then be reduced to an enforceable, written agreement. In a perfect world mediation sessions are concluded in one day.

Venue selection and choice of law provisions are standard provisions in franchise agreements regardless of whether the dispute is to be litigated in court, arbitrated or mediated.

Venue selection and choice of law provisions are standard provisions in franchise agreements regardless of whether the dispute is to be litigated in court, arbitrated or mediated. These are just further examples of the franchisor determining the rules of engagement.

Some franchise agreements provide that each party shall have a "champion" arbitrator who then selects a third impartial arbitrator to conduct the proceeding. Each party is responsible for the fees of his/her own arbitrator plus one-half of the fees of the neutral arbitrator. As arbitrators are often retired judges or experienced franchisee attorneys, the hourly rates can be substantial.

Mediation Is a Cost-Effective Process

Unlike arbitration, which may become quite protracted and expensive, mediation is recognized as a very cost-effective method to resolve a franchise dispute. Mediation is normally completed, whether successful or not, in one or two sessions. When successful, the parties avoid the expensive aspects of litigation, including extensive pleadings, discovery, dispositive motions (motions to dismiss and motions for summary judgment), trials and appeals. Even if the process is not successful, the parties have wasted little time or resources in attempting to resolve the dispute at an early stage. Further, the information gleaned through the process may prove helpful in future litigation as the decision-making persons for each party have been able to see, listen to and evaluate the credibility of potential witnesses and the strengths and weaknesses of their respective positions. Franchisees will end up spending much more money once they enter the litigation arena. It may be worthwhile to pursue mediation, especially if the parties believe the relationship will continue after the dispute is resolved. Mediation is usually less confrontational than arbitration or litigation, thus allowing the parties to go forward without any (or reduced) lingering anger towards one another.

Mediation Is a Collaborative and Creative Process

In order for mediation to be successful, the parties collaborate to ultimately create a resolution that will end the dispute. While the process is still adversarial, the setting is designed to remove the parties' confrontational attitudes and replace them (knowingly or unknowingly) with a willingness to structure a fair resolution. Mediation allows the parties to be creative in reaching a resolution; it goes beyond (or perhaps around, over or under) a determination of right and wrong to seek a *win-win* situation. Franchising is actually quite receptive to creative solutions, as the franchisor has many so-called "lollipops" he/she can provide the franchisee other than outright damages. These lollipops can include reduction of royalties or advertising fees for a period of time, concessions on product prices, extensions of terms, additional advertising or promotional assistance, management assistance, and preference on future expansion opportunities. All of these creative solutions may provide a benefit to the franchisee without requiring the franchisor to make direct payment of damages to the franchisee. If the parties can collaborate to forge a creative solution to the dispute, both sides can move forward without the need for extended litigation.

Mediation Is a Voluntary and Non-Binding Controlled Process

The parties ultimately control the mediation process. They enter it voluntarily, have a role in the mediator selection process and are not at risk of being bound by a bad decision or judgment. The mediator does not have any authority to enter a binding decision. At worst, the parties agree to disagree, and continue their dispute in another venue. At best, the parties successfully reach resolution of the dispute. Obviously, for the process to be worthwhile, each party must truly be desirous of achieving resolution of the dispute.

> *There is no guarantee that mediation will result in a binding resolution of the franchise dispute.*

The Disadvantages of Using Mediation To Resolve Franchise Disputes

In accordance with the battlefield analogy, one noted mediator usually begins his mediation session by telling the parties, "There is a bomb in the middle of this room, and every party has a trigger." There is no guarantee that mediation will result in a binding resolution of the franchise dispute, and the element of control provided to each party indeed may cause the mediation process to explode at any moment. Either party can "just say no" and end the process at any time. This then raises a legitimate franchisee premediation concern as to whether the process will be a complete waste of valuable time and limited resources. Mediation must be considered in comparison with other available avenues of resolution—namely litigation or arbitration.

The Mediator Has No Authority to Bind Parties

> *The potential success of mediation is dependent upon the mediator's ability to keep the parties at the table.*

Unlike a judge or arbitrator, the mediator has no power to issue a decision that is binding upon the parties. If the parties cannot agree on a resolution, there is no resolution. The potential success of mediation is dependent upon the mediator's ability to keep the parties at the table. If one of the parties has no real interest in resolving the issue in dispute, the mediator is powerless. Thus, the franchisee must give serious consideration as to whether the franchisor is serious about resolving the dispute or is just playing power games with the franchisee. Those franchise systems with an egotistical one-person show at the head of the franchise system are not as likely to treat mediation in a serious manner. In a trial or arbitration proceeding however, the franchisor's arrogance can come back to bite him in a jury verdict or judgment. And mediation has no mechanism to turn a franchisor's arrogance against him/her.

Another consideration is whether the issue in dispute is capable of being resolved by mediation. A system-wide attack which threatens to destroy the franchisor is probably not a good case for mediation. The franchisee must evaluate the nature of the dispute and his/her prior working relationship with the franchisor to determine whether mediation presents a probable likelihood for resolution of the dispute. Attorneys will be able to provide "war stories" of how they achieved a resolution through mediation of very dire franchise situations. For example, mediation has been used successfully to restore a terminated franchisee to a franchise system. Thus, mediation may work in even the most troublesome cases. However, the franchisee must consider whether, based on its experience, the franchisor is likely to fully commit to the resolution of the issue in dispute in a mediation proceeding.

Limited Weapons at the Franchisee's Disposal

Discovery may uncover that the franchisor has a prior history of mistreating other franchisees in the same, illegal manner.

It is important to note that mediation does not provide opportunity for a franchisee to conduct discovery (other than by listening carefully during the sessions). Discovery is a major means for a franchisee to increase his/her arsenal of weapons to use against the franchisor. Discovery may uncover that the franchisor has a prior history of mistreating other franchisees in the same, illegal manner and provide documentation and/or deposition testimony to support the franchisee's position. If the franchisee has stand-alone claims that scream injustice without need for further collaborative proof, then mediation may be an appropriate dispute resolution process. Otherwise franchisees may be depriving themselves of a valuable litigation tool that could enhance their likelihood of success.

Potential Avenue for Franchisor Abuse

By disclosing all franchisee claims and strategy in mediation, the franchisor will be able to devise strategic plans to thwart the franchisee's arguments at trial.

In addition to exhausting the franchisee's limited financial resources, the franchisor may use the mediation process as a means of unearthing the franchisee's trial strategy. By disclosing all franchisee claims and strategy in mediation, the franchisor will be able to devise strategic plans to thwart the franchisee's arguments at trial. While mediation is confidential and under rules of evidence statements made in mediation may not be used in court, this does not preclude the franchisor from seeking post-mediation discovery (i.e., such as bank records, tax returns, second set of books) that may confirm the damaging statements made at the mediation proceeding.

Thus, if a franchisee does not believe a franchisor wants the mediation to be successful, he/she should use caution in deciding how much of his/her case to disclose during mediation and how many of his/her weapons to hold in reserve for future engagements. The franchisor has much more experience in the mediation process and will be very careful in choosing what, if any, information it discloses to franchisees.

Conclusion

In selecting its modus operandi for dispute resolution, the franchisor has done everything in his/her power to create a battlefield providing him/her with the greatest advantage and chance of success. This chapter is a map of battlefield landmine locations. Learning the map is an important part of approaching any impending battle with franchisors.

If your present franchise agreement does not contain an ADR provision, there is a strong likelihood that, upon renewal, the new, then current franchise agreement will include an ADR provision.

CHAPTER IV
SALE OF EXISTING
FRANCHISED PROPERTY

Franchisees can make money two ways: (1) operating a franchise and (2) selling it. More than 500 books have been written on how to buy a new franchise and operate a franchise successfully. Except for occasional references to the need for estate planning, the focus of the attention on franchising is almost exclusively on the sale of new properties—the *primary* market. In contrast, there is a noticeable absence of written materials on how to sell franchises in the *secondary* market—that is, how to sell franchise properties that currently exist.

While the franchise industry as a whole has been mushrooming over the past 20 years, the infrastructure for resale has barely taken root.

There are currently about 620,000 franchise properties/units in the United States, and 10–15 percent, or 62,000–93,000 different franchised units, are available for sale at any given time. Many franchisees opened one or more of these properties/units while in their early 30s or 40s—some 10 or 20 years ago—and are now approaching retirement age. This overall aging of franchisee bodies is an obvious development which franchisors are beginning to notice. While the franchise industry as a whole has been mushrooming over the past 20 years, the infrastructure for resale has barely taken root.

Few franchisors have formal exit programs or even want to deal with the 10 to 15 percent of their existing franchisees seeking buyers. Until recently, franchisors appeared to focus almost exclusively on the sale of new properties/units, leaving the process of the sale of existing franchise properties/units unstructured. Even today, franchisors may or may not assist in the transfer of ownership from one franchisee to another. Judging from articles written by consultants in the franchise industry on the subject, the notion that a sound resale program maintains the market value of the entire system is struggling to gain widespread acceptance among franchisors.

Local business brokers may not have experience in selling existing franchises. Some brokers avoid franchise sales because they have the idea that such sales involve small amounts of money or due to the complexities resulting from the involvement of a third party (i.e., the franchisor's right of first refusal or the franchisor's right to approve or disqualify a buyer).

Financing is not readily available. Until recently, financial institutions, especially banks, were frequently reluctant to finance franchise business due to lack of familiarity with their nature. In addition, local banks were usually only willing to finance franchise properties in the state where their bank was established. This made it impossible to get a bank loan if the franchisee lived in one state while the salable properties were in another. It also posed a barrier for the multi-unit operator with properties in several states.

Local attorneys may or may not have the specialized expertise or experience necessary to structure a franchise sale. So how is the need for assistance in the sale of existing franchises being met?

The potential resources that do exist are not well known at a national level. For example, in the franchise resale or secondary market, there is no national equivalent of a Coldwell Banker or ERA Network, as there is in real estate. Moreover, the technological equivalent to a real estate multi-listing service for franchise resale is just now evolving on the internet.

In addition, the resale efforts of professionals appear to be more fragmented and driven by concept. A broker specializing in a specific fast food franchise chain, for example, may not sell hotel franchises. Further fragmentation results simply from geography. The person who sells existing franchises in New York probably does not make sales in California. Lastly, fragmentation results from the variety of resale professionals who operate in the secondary market. Accountants, attorneys, real estate brokers, business brokers, or investment bankers may all work the franchise resale market, depending upon the state requirements in which the franchise is located.

> ### *The franchisee may wait too long to start the resale process and then is overly eager to have the sale completed.*

In the absence of information, when the franchisee begins the resale process, he/she typically figures out, unscientifically and somewhat randomly, what to do just by doing. He/she also frequently learns, through expensive hindsight, what not to do. The franchisee may wait too long to start the resale process and then is overly eager to have the sale completed, not realizing that a well-executed sale process may take months.

> ### *Buying a franchise is typically a once-in-a-lifetime experience; so is its resale.*

Buying a franchise is typically a once-in-a-lifetime experience; so is its resale. Given the once-in-a-lifetime nature of the experience, the franchisee is at a distinct disadvantage if he/she has limited information of what to expect during the different stages of the reselling process. Just as mistakes in the operation of the business can cost the franchisee profitability, mistakes can also be very costly in the sale of the franchise.

One person described the sale of his existing franchises as a poker game—except that the stakes were very, very high. Knowing that three of a kind beats two pair is probably a good thing when betting on an investment that took years to mature and develop. It is probably best to know the rules of the game before the gambling begins.

The purpose of this chapter, then, is to give franchisees an overview of the sale process, outline alternatives, highlight key legal issues and provide specific information on available resources—all to help the franchisee achieve his/her desired outcome. Because the subject is complex and laws vary from state-to-state, the information here is a general overview. The first part deals with practical management issues; the second part deals with specific legal issues involved in the sale of existing franchises. Armed with an overview and specialized legal insight, the franchisee can then seek out appropriate information relevant to his/her unique situation when the resale process is undertaken.

THE SALES PROCESS

Making the Decision

Just like everyone else, franchisees get older, may become senile and eventually die. Some marriages end. Adult children may marry spouses who don't want to be involved in the business or may be interested, but lack the talent or drive to succeed in it.

Like Sisyphus in the Greek legend, the franchisee may grow weary of the unending task of rolling a rock up the hill, only to have it slide back down.

Some franchise systems go haywire and become self-destructive or litigious. Mid-life crises may dictate change or a different use of one's remaining years. New business opportunities beckon. Franchisees get tired of fixing problems, some of which may not stay fixed. Like Sisyphus in the Greek legend, the franchisee may grow weary of the unending task of rolling a rock up the hill, only to have it slide back down.

Like non-franchise business owners, franchisees frequently procrastinate and avoid dealing with their own retirement, potential disability or need for a succession plan. The franchisee lives as if the day will never come when transition will be necessary. According to this thinking, since the franchisee isn't selling now, he/she assumes that planning for resale may be postponed indefinitely. There may also be what turns out to be unrealistic hopes that family members will one day take over. According to SBA studies, only 25 percent of family-owned business pass to the next generation. Having a family member take over frequently turns out to be more of a dream than reality. Even worse, if the family member does take over and fails, the dream turns into a nightmare, and a *distress* sale becomes necessary.

Prior to resale, it is common for the franchisee to have considered alternatives, including hiring a manager at an acceptable level of compensation and stepping back to enjoy a leisurely routine. Such attempts frequently fail—not for lack of good intentions by the replacement, but simply because the franchisee/owner usually brings to the task a set of skills, a total commitment and a perspective that a paid manager lacks. When that alley turns out to be a dead-end, the franchisee frequently is forced to consider resale.

The decision to sell is usually triggered by one or more precipitating factors, not uncommonly involving major life changes. Examples include:

- Desire for leisure or retirement.
- Lack of successor or loss of key member of business without viable replacement.
- Divorce from a spouse who played a key role in the operation.
- Need to diversify; desire for more liquid assets.
- Disability or death of the franchisee.
- Emotional burn-out (i.e., loss of desire to continue in business or a sense that new "blood" or new energy could result in growth).
- Concerns with the direction of the franchise system encroachment, labor shortages or cost of materials increasing.

- Increases in leases or taxes, new ownership of franchise system.
- Operational problems or saturation of the market by competition or the imposition of franchisor-rules or policies which negatively impact franchisees, etc.
- Interest in new business opportunity elsewhere.
- Turn-around profit strategy (the franchise purchased the business at a discount, optimized its performance and now wants to resell at a profit).
- Declining profitability due to increasingly adverse retail conditions (for example, deterioration of a shopping center).

The franchisee who waits to sell until he/she is desperate is at a tremendous disadvantage in the negotiating process.

Whatever the reason for sale, the franchisee (or the heirs, in the case of the franchisee's death) can enhance the goal of optimizing the investment by proceeding methodically—by "making haste . . . slowly." However urgent the desire to sell the franchise business, planning and preparation are\ needed. The franchisee who waits to sell until he/she is desperate is at a tremendous disadvantage in the negotiating process. A buyer may sense the desperation and may respond in two ways—making a lowball offer or backing away from the deal entirely. The seller needs to approach the process with a split mentality. In other words, he/she needs to operate the franchise as if it will not be sold, and remain emotionally committed to its success, while simultaneously working very hard to prepare the business for a sale.

The selling process begins only after the preparation is completed.

When painting a room, the professional painter doesn't start to paint until the walls are prepared, the outlets and fixtures removed, the surface clean and absorbent, protective drop cloths are laid on the carpet, the paint has been purchased and stirred and the tools, including ladders and rollers, are assembled. So, too, with the sale of the franchise. The selling process begins only after the preparation is completed.

Preparation

Selling a franchised business is a lot of work, usually piled on top of an already demanding work schedule. It is reassuring to note, however, that the list of tasks needing completion is definite. The most obvious tasks are:

Decide What to Sell: Depending on the legal structure of the entity and the possible role of the franchisor in the approval process, the franchisee may want to sell assets only, sell common stock (if corporation) or exchange stock (if both buyer and seller are corporations). The overriding consideration may be taxes, because if a corporation sells its assets, it risks double taxation. Taxes may need to be paid on the capital gains to the corporation on the sale of assets, then, when the money reaches the stock owner, either in the form of wages, dividends or bonuses, the stock owner is personally taxed a second tax. The advantage of trading stock (if the buyer has stock which is marketable, such as publicly traded stock) is that taxes can be deferred by the seller until an advantageous time. Here's where a good accountant can save a franchisee money by helping work through the tax implications of various strategies. Of course, a buyer's offer may cause the issue to be revisited, but this preliminary work is still useful.

> *It is not uncommon for franchisees, like other businesspeople, to use the business to support a personal lifestyle—travel, benefits, salary, etc.*

Recast Financial Statements: It is not uncommon for franchisees, like other businesspeople, to use the business to support a personal lifestyle—travel, benefits, salary, etc.—which also has the benefit of minimizing taxes. If these lifestyle elements have been buried in financial statements, it is best to clean up the statements prior to a sale. Otherwise, the franchisee will need to prepare revised financial statements—with appropriate justifications for every expense taken out. Other items besides owners' compensation that could be adjusted include: depreciation and amortization, interest and debt service. If, for example, the franchise is sold for a multiple of five times cash flow, every dollar that the seller can add back in is worth five at the time of sale. Knowledge of the impact of this formula provides a real incentive to re-work the financial statements.

In addition to recasting prior financial statements, the franchisee may want to prepare a three-year projection, after having made the adjustments, to give a prospective buyer an idea of what the future holds. The franchisee may also want to prepare a list of key ratios used in the particular franchise system, i.e., cost of labor to sales, standard profit margins, cost of materials relative to sales, percentage of sales allocated to advertising, the amount of royalties relative to sales, etc.—so the prospective buyer can review the financial statements with these yardsticks in mind.

This is also the time to separate personal assets so they are not included in the resale and to pay off any shareholder loans. For store and restaurant owners who rent space, it may also be time to close any unit that is failing so the remaining units are even more profitable. The franchisee also needs to become current on accounts payable, accounts receivable and inventory management; this is especially true with any outstanding obligations to the franchisor.

Just as a house is dressed up before being offered for sale, the franchise properties/units need to be cleaned, fixed and repaired.

Upgrade Facilities: Just as a house is dressed up before being offered for sale, the franchise properties/units need to be cleaned, fixed and repaired. If remodeling to current franchisor standards is not financially possible or would involve an amount of money not likely to be recovered in the resale, a franchisee might want to limit work to painting, cleaning, organizing and making other cosmetic changes. Entrances, landscaping, offices, customer lobbies, break rooms—the better they look, the better a seller's chances of receiving full value without having to discount the sale price. The intent here is to produce a positive impact on the buyer when the franchised businesses are shown while minimizing the expense.

Codify Procedures: The key parts of the business—like personnel policies—must be in writing. Develop a manual that outlines key processes and timelines. Include information systems; key financial controls; and marketing, communication and public relations practices and programs.

Organize Records: Clean up and organize files. Make sure all necessary documentation is in place from governmental agencies (ERISA, OSHA, EEOC, EPA, workers' compensation claims and unemployment claims). Make sure all entity documents (shareholder meeting minutes, for example) are current and complete. Systematize tax records and filings so they are easily available for review. Organize all real estate leases and contracts binding the company. Locate and have available payroll records, franchise agreements, loan documents, accounting ledgers, financial statements and advertising/marketing contracts. Many of these documents will have to be reproduced or reviewed, so having them organized and immediately available saves time and strain.

> *The life of each lease is critical to the sale of the franchise.*

Review Leases: The life of each lease is critical to the sale of the franchise. If a lease has limited time left, without a provision for renewal, the seller may want to renegotiate a new lease with the landlord, thereby assuring continuous operation of the franchise business. In some instances, landlords may be willing to break an existing lease if incentivized—either by higher rent now or in the future or by extending the lease over a longer period of time (i.e. replacing a lease with 18 months left with a five-year-lease with option to renew). Later in the process, the franchisee needs to make sure that the franchisor will release him/her from personal guarantees (if they have been required on leases) and replace them with those from the new buyer. If the franchisor won't agree to a replacement, then the purchase agreement must be written to include indemnification for this contingent liability.

> *As part of the resale strategy, the franchisee may want to consolidate the various businesses into one entity.*

Restructure Entities: While having common management, it is not uncommon for a multiple unit franchisee to have more than one legal entity involved. For example, the group might include several limited partnerships or, even more complex, might include one or more corporations, limited liability companies, limited partnerships or individual ownership with the common thread being the general management. As part of the resale strategy, the franchisee may want to consolidate the various businesses into one entity, thereby making it easier for a prospective buyer to understand the acquisition. Or, if the franchisee has a large chain with properties in different states, he/she might want to break up the single entity and sell off the chain in pieces, based on self-contained areas. Whether consolidating or breaking into parts, the franchisee needs to be aware of unexpected transaction costs resulting from the restructuring (i.e., sales taxes, depreciation recapture, etc.). Care also must be taken to communicate internally to investors or other partners with equity interests so that necessary approvals and support for the strategy—whether consolidation or spin-off—are obtained prior to execution. Finally, a franchisee should get good legal and accounting advice before taking any action in this area, to avoid possible major tax or other problems.

Organize Management Team: In multiple-property operations, the strength of the infrastructure is a major asset. A franchisee should be prepared to show it on paper. He/she should write out individual job responsibilities and detail delegations. He/she should develop an organization chart. He/she should build a management team that can take the company through a transition to new ownership.

This isn't a complete list, but is suggestive of the kinds of preparation that the franchisee needs to undertake as part of the sale process. Once the preparation is completed, a price needs to be assigned to the franchise business—a price which the franchisee can now justify in light of the quality of the business being offered for sale. This preparation may sound endless and overly comprehensive, but the steps are necessary to ensure the speed of the resale and the maximum resale price.

Placing a Value

The ultimate indicator of a business' value is the price a buyer will pay. The franchisee needs to have worked through different methodologies so he/she understands how each works and what the implications are for the dollar placed on the business. What doesn't work is for the franchisee to ask for a specific price based on an idiosyncratic rationale. Here are three examples of what *doesn't work* in setting a resale price:

Franchisee Efforts: In this approach, the franchisee calculates the dollars invested in the business and/or the time he/she has invested to get the business to its current level, then places a value accordingly. Unfortunately for the seller, it doesn't matter to a prospective buyer how hard the franchisee may have worked in the past, or that it required an investment of $500,000 to get a single property to profitability. All that matters is the present and future direction of present earnings and profitability—*sweat equity* typically can't be included in the pricing formula.

Sales Levels: Unless supported by profitability, sales levels typically aren't used as a basis for sale. Continued sales growth can be justification for a certain price, but the presence of sales without corresponding profitability isn't likely to become the basis for the sales price.

Franchisee Need: The franchisee makes a decision on what he/she wants to net out of the business. This is like the employee who approaches the boss and says "I need a pay raise because I need another $200 to cover the payment on my new car." The employer is unlikely to set compensation based on the employee's need. Similarly, a franchise buyer is unlikely to purchase the business based on what the present owner needs to net out of it.

What *does* work are the following approaches, generally accepted throughout the business community:

Asset Approach

> *The value of assets can be based on liquidation value, replacement cost value or fair market value.*

With this methodology, the franchisee lists assets (i.e. property, equipment, leasehold improvements, goodwill, inventory), totals them and offers them for sale. The value of assets can be based on liquidation value, replacement cost value, or fair market value. This approach is useful when there are significant tangible assets and also when properties/units are not profitable. For example, if a franchisee has three properties/units up and running but not yet profitable, using a multiple of the profits would make the franchises worthless. Instead, the seller will need to use an asset approach, arguing that replacement costs reflect the true value of the franchise unit/property. In this example, if it typically costs $150,000 to get a franchise unit/property open and to bring sales up to $30,000/month, then $150,000 is the replacement value, or sale price, for this unit/property.

Comparison Approach

In this model, the sales price is based on other units sold in the same franchise chain. Analysis of units/properties with similar sales and profits is required with this approach. In real estate, this is referred to as *comparables*. When a residential real estate broker prepares to list a home for sale, typically, the broker will generate a list of *comparables* in order to put a price on the sale of the home. Homes will be matched by number of bedrooms, square footage, neighborhood, etc.

> *If the franchise operated more profitably than the franchise standard, value would go up.*

This approach can also be used in the resale of a franchise. For example, if franchise properties typically sell for $500,000 when sales and profits reach a specified level, then the franchisee can assume that he/she could set the price accordingly for the property being resold. Other factors, however, also serve to increase or decrease the price. If the franchise operated more profitably than the franchise standard, value would go up. Other factors that might merit a premium price include, sales increasing faster than the system average, opportunity for major expansion market dominance, exceptionally well-operated properties, etc. Other factors might have a mitigating or negative effect. These include, no room for expansion, major remodeling requirements, declining sales, a reputation for poorly managed units, overwhelming competition, etc. In addition, for this approach to work, it is important to have standardized and validated financial information on similar franchise properties or industry units on which to make comparisons. Unfortunately, this information may be difficult to obtain.

Income Capitalization Approach

With this approach, a value is placed on the present worth of the future economic benefits to the prospective buyer. A *payback* period is assumed. A future income stream is projected over that period, then the earnings are discounted back to present value, using a competitive discount rate with investments of comparable risk. The discount takes into account inflation, the cost of money and the inherent risks of the investment. Specialized software is available to assist with this kind of calculation. Like all other calculations, the resulting numbers are a function of what factors are fed into the formula. Obviously, this approach assumes a current profit that can be projected into the future. If the business has a declining profit, the methodology works to the disadvantage of the seller. This methodology is commonly used by the buyer to assess the rate of return given the price being asked on the business. For that reason, the seller needs to be familiar with the approach and understand its implications.

A variation on this approach commonly accepted by both buyers and sellers uses a multiple of cash flow to set the price. If the seller in a particular franchise industry typically receives three to five times cash flow after making adjustments, this multiple is used as a guide in setting the price. This approach is meaningful to many buyers because income generation is tangible. Obviously, the multiple that is used is the deciding factor here, and the selling franchisee needs to establish the common denominator in his/her franchise industry as part of the process of setting the price. Moreover, if this approach is used, then it is critical that the seller make the adjustments referred to in the section on recasting financial statements. Every dollar put back in is multiplied and reflected in the sale price.

Setting an asking price involves as much art as math.

Setting an asking price involves as much art as math. If the price is unrealistically high, prospective buyers are turned off. The longer the franchise is for sale, the more likely the word will spread among potential buyers that the offer is tainted. Equally disconcerting, the more time passes, the more likely it is that employees will get wind of the prospective sale and begin jumping the ship. On the other hand, a price *too low* signals distress and will attract *bottom-fishers*, one of the least attractive buyers. A *too low* price may also send the message that there is something seriously wrong with the business, even though the price would represent a bargain. In any event, the franchisee needs to make sure the asking price is supported by a rational and accepted methodology. The seller needs to understand the methodology so it can be explained completely to the potential buyer. The buyer may not agree with the resulting figure, he/she will understand how the franchisee arrived at the value so that further dialogue can occur.

The franchisee needs to make sure that the asking price is supported by a rational and accepted methodology.

Marketing/Advertising

Selling a franchise business has elements common to the sale of any business, but it also has some unique characteristics. In addition to selling the specifics of his/her business to a buyer, the franchisee must also:

Sell the buyer on the value of the *franchise concept* as well as the health and vitality of the franchise system. For example, if the franchise system is receiving negative publicity as a result of lawsuits from disgruntled existing or former franchisees, the sale of the franchise becomes more difficult.

Sell the buyer on the *industry*. Again, if the industry overall is suffering from a glut of competition or declining due to obsolescence, selling the franchise is more difficult. It is still possible to sell the franchise—it is just that more effort will likely be needed to find a buyer.

Sell the buyer on the advantages of an *established* vs. a new franchise. Those advantages can be:

- Less risk—starting out with an operating history vs. gambling on new units/properties.
- Easier financing—a company with a current profit is easier to finance than one with projections only.
- The benefits of past efforts—currently established leases and franchise agreements are possibly now more advantageous than new ones. Also, products or services are already known as a result of past advertising in the market.

Sell the buyer on the *market* in which the franchises are located. The seller can promote the availability of expansion sites or prospects for continued growth with existing units/ properties. If the seller shares the market with other franchisees, he/she can promote the collegial relationships of the surrounding franchises as well as any mechanism in place for shared governance of common areas of concern, such as advertising pools, expansion policies, training, etc. Incidentally, it is good to have all fences mended before selling this point to a buyer.

Sell the franchisor on the *qualifications* of the buyer so the franchisor does not block the sale.

Not incidentally, the franchisee first needs to make sure that he/she has something to sell. The franchise agreement either needs to be renewed, renewable, assignable, or *evergreen*—continuing in perpetuity assuming future franchisor requirements are met. If the agreement is about to end and there is no renewal, then the buyer does not have time to recoup his/her investment, and the resale will be thwarted.

The franchisee also needs to review the franchise agreement to see whether the franchisor:

- Has the option to purchase the business.
- Has the right of first refusal.
- Has requirements or conditions that must be met in order to give approval for the sale.
- Included fees with obtaining the transfer of ownership.
- Has other specific requirements.

The franchisor is likely to require that the franchisee be in full compliance with the franchise agreement and have no outstanding debts to the franchisor or its affiliates. The franchisor will also want assurance that the buyer is competent to run the company and that the operation of the properties/units will be continuous with no business interruption. The franchisor may also have a transfer fee, specified training requirements of the buyer and require that units be upgraded/remodeled. If the franchise is not evergreen and has a limited life, the selling franchisee will need to renegotiate the agreement so the buying franchisee can sign a new agreement or extend the life of the existing franchise agreement. The use of a new franchise agreement also may trigger disclosure requirements on the part of the franchisor which impact the sale.

Perhaps the hardest decision for the franchisee to make is how to advertise the franchise for sale without disrupting current operations. This is particularly true for the multi-unit franchisee who needs continuity in his/her management infrastructure. The franchisee also has to decide whether to market the business himself/herself (a direct sale) or turn the sale over to a third party (an indirect sale) using the services of specialists in franchise resales—attorneys, accountants, general business brokers, or investment bankers. Either approach, selling directly to a buyer or indirectly through the use of a third party, can be used, and each has distinct advantages and disadvantages. The franchisee also has to make a decision at which point a candid discussion with the franchisor, who will be party to the sale, should occur.

If the franchisee decides to sell the business directly to a buyer, then the initial strategy requires drawing up a list of potential buyers within the franchisee's own network. In coming up with the list, the franchisee may consider selling the business to a key employee. Typically, this employee knows the business and is often qualified from the franchisor's perspective. The downside is that the employee usually doesn't have money. Payment for the business must often come from existing cash flow over some period of time.

Too little oversight may cause the franchisee to be blind to impending disaster.

The seller is still on the hook in terms of liability and may find it emotionally difficult to let go while retaining some degree of oversight during the transition period. Too little oversight may cause the franchisee to be blind to impending disaster. Too much oversight handcuffs the new manager/owner. In the event the key employee is unable to manage the business successfully, the franchisee may have a tough time regaining control of the business. Psychologically, it is also extremely difficult to let a business go and then recover the drive, energy and enthusiasm to rebuild it. Moreover, from a legal perspective, unless the failure is well-documented, charges and countercharges may result in a messy and expensive lawsuit.

Also, looking internally, the franchisee may want to consider an investor or equity partner who would like to have total ownership. If the franchisee has had the foresight to set up a *buy/sell* agreement, then this agreement can provide an exit for the franchisee who is disabled, or for his/her heirs if the franchisee dies. In this arrangement, the agreement for one partner to buy and the other partner to sell is triggered by predetermined conditions, such as disability or death. Insurance taken out as part of the agreement can be used to pay the selling partner for his/her ownership interests. The departing partner or the heirs receive cash and the business is now totally owned by the remaining partner.

If such arrangements haven't been made in advance, or if death or disability is not the trigger for the decision to sell, an internal sale can still occur, though the price must be negotiated. Moreover, the selling partner may have to take back *paper* if the buying partner has insufficient capital and cannot obtain financing. In this case, besides having the business as collateral, the selling partner will probably also want to set up a life insurance policy on the new owner/partner, making the selling partner the beneficiary as part of the condition of a loan.

> *The franchisee association, if one exists, may be a source for names of franchisees who are expanding.*

Looking outside the company, the selling franchisee wants to consider adjacent franchisees or other franchisees in the market, another franchisee elsewhere in the system who would like entrance into the market, or franchisees in an expansion mode— assuming they are in *good standing* with the franchisor. The franchisee association, if one exists, may be a source for names of franchisees who are expanding.

Selling to an existing franchisee has an advantage in that the franchisor's cooperation is more likely assured. But a word of caution needs to be added here. If a neighboring franchisee covets a territory and knows of the desire to sell, he/she could take steps to block the sale or make it difficult, then wait for the business to fail and buy the territory from the franchisor, presumably for much less than buying the existing business. The neighboring franchisee may also market more aggressively into the territory, knowing that attention is being diverted elsewhere.

The franchisor may also be a potential buyer.

The franchisor may also be a potential buyer, depending upon his/her current mode—whether he/she is acquiring and converting franchisee units to franchisor-owned or whether the franchisor is selling off company-owned properties. Even where the franchisor is acquiring properties, however, the price offered is likely to be less than what could be realized through the sale to a third party. It is not in the best interest of the franchisor to outbid other franchisees, and create conflict within the system. Consequently, the franchisor will tend to be the *buyer of last resort*. If the franchisee cannot sell the units/properties elsewhere, the franchisor may be willing, in some cases, such as fast food chains, to buy the units/properties, but at a reduced price. In this case, the franchisor may offer cash or stock, which if publicly traded, is convertible to cash. In addition, the franchisor can remove all contingent liability. These are both strong reasons to consider an offer from the franchisor, if one is made.

Vendors who have a significant interest in the success of the franchise may also be potential buyers. In addition, executives within the franchisor's corporate office who have an entrepreneurial flair may also be enticed to operate their own franchise as opposed to being in a corporate role—particularly if they have gained experience operating company-owned units/properties.

In that case, a buyout over time could be structured. This arrangement, however, could involve risk both to the franchisee (the franchisor may squelch the deal and punish the franchisee for attempting to steal a valued employee) and to the buyer (the employee may be fired simply for engaging in discussions to buy out the franchisee, whether or not those negotiations come to fruition).

The franchisee's accountant or attorney may have leads on prospective buyers.

Although competitors might like to get their hands on certain properties/units (especially in the fast food industry), they are not likely to be approved by the franchisor as potential buyers. The franchisee's accountant or attorney may have leads on prospective buyers as might local attorneys and/or accountants in the franchise community. Networking among the franchisee's own extended family, friends and professional associates may also generate leads.

In approaching different parties, the franchisee has to make assessments about the reliability of the buyer in terms of maintaining confidentiality. Full use of confidentiality agreements is recommended. The franchisee should also do some serious investigation to make sure any prospective buyers that surface have the financial qualifications to execute a sale before the franchise releases significant financial information. He/she will also need to be satisfied that the buyer has the capability to manage the business. The franchisee also needs to qualify the buyer with response to employees, should word of the resale efforts reach the organization. An example of such a response might be setting up a special termination bonus if an employee remains throughout the sale process.

Qualifying a buyer can be done a number of ways, first by requesting a current personal and/or business financial statement. Verification of assets listed either on the personal or business financial statement can also be requested, along with individual or business tax returns. In addition to the personal financial statement, the franchisee can verify cash to be used for the down payment through review of notarized bank statements. Later in the process, when the sale becomes more likely, the franchisee may ask the buyer to provide a letter from the financing institution, verifying intent to finance. Beware of the buyer who waves off the question of how payment will be made until the end of the deal. The franchisee must be assured in the early stages of negotiation—before releasing information and risking exposure and loss of key employees—that the buyer has the means to effect a sale.

Early on, it is important to talk with the franchisor about the potential sale and then keep the franchisor updated as appropriate. Most likely, the franchisor will not have a formally structured resale program. That doesn't mean, however, that he/she can't be of considerable assistance. The franchisor can provide promotional materials to share with prospective buyers. He/she also may be willing to provide names of existing franchisees who are in an acquisition mode. In addition, by having continuous dialogue early on, the franchisee can surface and work through any franchisor-imposed impediments to the sale.

The seller may also need to arrange for a potential buyer to be given certain franchisor documents—even if the buyer is a current franchisee.

Since no one likes unpleasant surprises, the likelihood of obtaining the franchisor's cooperation is enhanced when the franchisor is involved in the process. It is also useful to have an executive in the franchisor's office serving as the franchisee's partner in the sale process. He/she can validate the strength of the franchise concept, the future growth plans of the system and the future for the industry within which the franchise operates and provide suitable supportive materials. The seller may also need to arrange for a potential buyer to be given certain franchisor documents—even if the buyer is a current franchisee. If the buyer is not a current franchisee, then he/she may also need to complete franchisor-mandated training, the cost of which is a point to be negotiated in the sale.

> *The franchisor may be willing to play a facilitative role between franchisees who are buying and selling units/properties.*

The franchisor might be willing, upon request, to divert some of its leads or sales prospects to the franchisee seller—particularly if a prospective buyer is interested in expansion and could use the existing property/unit(s) as a base from which to branch out. Such an arrangement would make it easier for a *new* franchisee to acquire financing, meet the franchisor's needs for expansion and create an exit for the selling franchisee. By partnering an experienced franchisee with a new entrant, success is more likely. Also, the franchisor may be willing to play a facilitative role between franchisees who are buying and selling units/properties in several markets in order to consolidate markets. It doesn't hurt to remind the franchisor of the benefits of having solid exit strategies for the company's existing franchisees—it enhances the value of other units and assures potential investors of the possibility of liquidity when it is time to sell.

If the threat of employees leaving once they learn of the potential sale of the franchise is not an issue, or if the franchisee is the owner/operator with few, if any, employees, then the franchisee might want to consider advertising the business in appropriate publications and newspapers. This may be the preferred method for a single property franchisee since it is difficult to command the resources of a major broker for a small transaction. Some franchisors have restrictions on the nature of advertising. For example, *Hotel for Sale* may be permitted while the name of the specific franchise, *Ashbury Suites*, may not. Moreover, qualifying the buyers for a small purchase is a major headache since only one or two potential buyers out of hundreds of responses may be qualified.

Another possibility to consider is listing the business on national listing services, such as Business Resale Network on the internet, a company affiliated with *Entrepreneur* magazine. This listing-only service has, on the average, 4,000 businesses with about 1,000 of those being franchise properties/units. Buyer inquiries can have the properties/units sorted by type or kind, geography, price, etc., and the number of hits has climbed to 1,500 per day, many of which are broker inquiries. The selling franchisees pay a fee for the listing service for three or six months.

Obviously, in using this service, confidentiality is either waived or maintained by arranging to have calls diverted either to the franchisor who can qualify the leads, to a broker who can serve as a buffer or to the franchisee who can screen the call. Of course, if enough information is provided in the listing, an enterprising employee may be able to figure out which properties/units are for sale despite these strategies. The advantage of using the service is national exposure to potential buyers. The listing service may be better suited for smaller franchisees, where word getting out about the proposed sale is not as major a consideration as it is for the multi-property/unit franchisee selling the management infrastructure as well as the individual properties/units.

The professional also serves as a buffer in smoothing out the rough spots in the road.

Specialists in the secondary franchise sales market—attorneys, accountants, investment bankers and business brokers—may be particularly useful when multiple units are being marketed. The franchisee may get the advantage of experience and skills, particularly in negotiating; objectivity; access to buyers; and assurance of confidentiality. Because the professional acts as a third party in the deal and can maintain confidentiality, the franchisee's management infrastructure is more likely to remain intact—a key part of the assets. The professional also serves as a buffer in smoothing out the rough spots in the road. Some or all of the following tasks may be performed by a third party professional:

- determining salability of business and value;
- developing a marketing strategy;
- preparing a "selling" document that provides all critical information about the business;
- initiating contact with potential buyers;
- evaluating buyers' financial soundness;
- maintaining confidentiality by being buffer until appropriate to reveal names;
- overseeing the process from beginning to end, including the acquisition and distribution of additional information;
- negotiating prices and other terms;
- arranging financing;
- serving as a liaison with the franchisor so impediments are removed;
- bringing the sale to closure;
- advising on tax and transition issues; and/or
- maintaining and administering escrow accounts, if necessary.

Laws governing the licensing requirements for professionals who can sell businesses vary from state to state. The selling franchisee needs to do research to find local, regional or national agents as well as find out what services are included in the fee and what their respective fee schedules are. If the professional does not provide key services (for example, locating buyers, arranging for financing or overseeing the process of obtaining franchisor approval), then the seller probably needs to keep searching. Also, don't assume that the professional you engage knows franchising in general or your particular franchise industry in particular. You may need to educate the professional if this is his/her first experience.

Where financing is involved, the down payment is commonly 20 to 30 percent of the purchase price. Taking *paper* in any form involves considerable risk to the franchisee. Should a selling franchisee have to come back and take over the business because of default, as much as half or more of the assets are likely to have been dissipated. The seller has to assess—on limited information over a limited period of time—the buyer's ability to run the business successfully in order to generate enough income to pay the note. Consequently, the selling franchisee will want security—including sold assets, inventory, ongoing receivables, other assets of the buyer, a personal guaranty, and/or personal assets of the guarantor. The security arrangements need to be fully documented and all appropriate steps taken to be sure security interests attach to the sale and can be executed should the need arise.

Getting all of the money out of the business and eliminating all contingency liability if the business fails are the major worries for most selling franchisees. To address these, one new company, National Franchise Sales, has introduced a resale program in the secondary market, promising *cash out without complications.* National Franchise Sales is headquartered in Norwalk, Connecticut and has four regional offices throughout the United States. Their *one stop* services include all of the preparatory work, locating buyers, obtaining franchisor approval, and arranging financing—even to the point of preparing a business plan for the buyer to qualify for SBA or other institutional loans. Because of its ongoing relationship with Deutsche Bank in particular and other financial institutions in general, National Franchise Sales is able to provide expedited financing, thereby allowing the franchisee to cash out. Using its services may provide franchisees—particularly those with multiple units—a clean way out.

The typical fee for professional services in resales varies and frequently is negotiable.

The typical fee for professional services in resales varies and frequently is negotiable. The range is usually 7 to 10 percent of the sales price, depending upon the size of the transaction. Usually, the smaller the transaction, the higher the fee. With larger transactions (as in the case with multiple units) the lower end of the scale applies. Whether using a local or national resource, the professional's track record and his/her particular specialized expertise in franchise resales needs to be verified before formalizing the relationship. In addition, the franchisee needs to make sure that the professional has access to financing—a factor which can be critical to the sale of the business.

Franchisees with multiple units need to give considerable thought to the decision to use a third party professional—particularly one who specializes in franchise resales—as opposed to attempting the sale on his/her own. Professional assistance may relieve the franchisee from considerable work, bring about multiple buyers, create a high sale price and leave the franchisee completely free of concern over the future health of the business.

> *Selling a franchised business is a lot like having a baby—it is hard to convey what the experience is like to someone who hasn't gone through it.*

Selling a franchised business is a lot like having a baby—it is hard to convey what the experience is like to someone who hasn't gone through it. The emotional toll is high, especially for franchisees who may be stressed for other reasons (e.g., poor health, poor finances, divorce or other family issues). Having a respected professional person serve as counselor, *reality check* and buffer can minimize the anguish. But whether using a specialist or going it alone, the franchisee needs to be prepared for the roller-coaster experience of the resale process.

The franchisee needs to allow sufficient time for the negotiation and sales process—months, not days. Pressure for a premature decision from the buyer can kill the deal or result in a lowered sales price. In addition, the amount of effort should not be underestimated—the franchisee must be prepared to heavily invest his/her own time over an extended period. This is *extra* work on top of the work of keeping the business running. The time will be spent preparing and reviewing documents for prospective buyers, consulting with the professionals (attorney, accountant, business brokers), talking with the franchisor, evaluating offers, etc. The franchisee needs to known it is not uncommon to have considered the business sold two or three times before it is finally done. Lastly, the franchisee needs to operate the business as if he/she will keep the business forever. To drop out psychologically because of a potential sale can be a costly mistake.

At some point in time, an offer will be made that can or will be accepted. In an ideal world, the franchisee obtains multiple offers and plays them off against each other. More likely, the offers will come in sequence. Whether or not any offer is acceptable is partly a function of the franchisee's negotiating skills. That is true whether he/she is negotiating directly or through a professional. Below are some key negotiating tips developed from others' experiences that might be useful to consider:

The franchisee must stay focused on big picture. He/she should not be offended when working through the details or waste time arguing about non-essential points. If a franchisee receives a *take it or leave it* offer, he/she may feel cheated out of the opportunity to present—with overpowering logic—why the business, based on valuation methodology, etc., merits a higher price. The franchisee should set feelings aside and objectively assess the offer in light of the larger goal—selling the business.

> *Be prepared for give and take. Keep emotions and ego at home.*

The selling franchisee should be prepared for give and take and keep emotions and ego at home. He/she should not be offended if the value placed on the business isn't as much as the buyer feels it is worth. Know personal limitations; get help from an attorney when legal issues are bogging the deal down or an accountant when financial issues are tangling up the deal.

> *The deal that looks dead one day may be alive the next. But the opposite is also true—the deal that is alive today may disappear tomorrow.*

Any offer received will probably seem too low; however, it may become an acceptable offer with offsetting factors. These may include cash instead of seller-financing, removal of contingent liability on leases or personal guarantees. So, the selling franchisee should avoid *take it or leave it* responses. And don't give up. Seemingly immovable obstacles have a way of disappearing when both parties are interested in consummating the deal. Each deal has a life and pattern of its own. The deal that looks dead one day may be alive the next. But the opposite is also true—the deal that is alive today may disappear tomorrow. Keeping steady in the midst of this turbulence is challenging, but necessary.

Pick up on the buyer's main goals so they can be reinforced in what you, the selling franchisee, offer. Franchisees may be able to include *extras* that cost little but mean a great deal to the buyer. It is important to let the buyer make the first offer so the seller can negotiate up. If the selling franchisee makes the first offer and it is less than what the buyer would have paid, the seller leaves money on the table.

The seller should be prepared to walk away from a deal. Knowing the option of declining the offer gives franchisees a tremendous advantage. But if they do walk away, they need to be prepared to live with the consequences. This is not a time to bluff. Attempting to restart negotiations after walking away once is a blow to a franchisee's credibility.

The seller should not hide the rocks under the water; they will come back to cut little feet. From a practical perspective, if anything comes out during the process that the franchisee hid, the deal will be tainted. Besides, the law requires full disclosure of all facts and circumstances that the seller knows are material to the buyer. In some states, the law may require full disclosure of all facts and circumstances that *would be* (as well as *are*) material to any buyer. Besides, operating with integrity establishes an atmosphere of trust and respect that is invaluable in working through the many obstacles that every deal encounters.

Don't push for the last nickel or dime. Stop when the deal is done.

Don't push for the last nickel or dime. Stop when the deal is done. Maintaining friendly relations goes a long way towards seeing a challenging process to conclusion. Be assured that there will be continuing opportunities for give and take until the entire matter is brought to closure.

It is also important to note that the price of the business is only one factor in whether the negotiations are successful. Other issues that must be addressed are: the tax implications, the effective date, the terms for payment (such as cash, stock for stock, promissory note, the interest on any notes, contingent payments or earn-outs), the role and terms of the selling franchisee's employment once sale has occurred, which assets are included in the sale vs. what is not included or sold separately, transition management, escrow provisions and the length of the non-compete clause, to name a few.

Payment for the business can be structured in several ways—cash, notes, stock, earn-outs or any combination of these. The timing of payment and interest on future payments are also key factors. The advantages and disadvantages of each payment method are illustrated in the chart on the next page.

If the franchisee is ever in the situation of having to come back in to take over the business, entering after default on payment, he/she has probably lost most of the investment.

If each of these categories wasn't complicated enough (payment in the form of stock is particularly complex) they may each be used in combination. The structure of the sale may involve cash down (typically 20/30 percent), a note payable out over time and stock.

Each of the elements has to be structured by the franchisee to minimize the risk. For example, the note payable over time could be secured by other assets of the buyer, so in the event the business fails, those assets could be used to cover the shortfall.

Otherwise, if the franchisee is ever in the situation of having to come back in to take over the business, entering after default on payment, he/she has probably lost most of the investment. Since the reason for default is a failed business, it is likely that there will not be much left to come back to. Moreover, if the franchisee accepts stock in the new company as payment and the new company fails, the new stock may have no value and the

	Advantages	Disadvantages
Cash	Completes deal for seller.	Immediate tax liabilities.
	Won't lose its value, like stock.	Requires handling and re-investment.
	Doesn't depend on future success of business.	Buyer may ask for discount in price.
		Buyer may have to arrange financing of remainder, which takes time or could be denied.
Notes	Defers tax liabilities, thereby postponing payment to an opportune time.	May be risky, depending upon qualifications of buyer.
	Can result in higher sales price.	May be dependent upon future performance of business.
	Increases range of potential buyers.	Ties up capital that could be invested for greater return elsewhere.
Stock	Increases range of potential buyers.	Increases risk, depending upon strength of stock.
	Defers taxes until stock sold.	May tie up capital if stock is not liquid; in fact, capital may never be available.
	Buyer could benefit on upside.	
	Can result in higher sales price.	
Earn-Outs	Increases number of buyers.	Is dependent upon success of business.
	Buyer could benefit on upside if linked to performance.	Buyer harmed by downside.
	Defers tax liability to opportune time.	Ties up investment capital.

investment could be lost. Investment expertise (as well as accounting and legal expertise) is required in the structuring of sales involving notes, stock and earn-outs because investment decisions, as well as business decisions, are being made.

Typically, once all these items are negotiated, the franchisee and buyer move to a letter of intent or a memorandum of understanding. That memo needs to include:

- Price and terms.
- Structure and payment.
- Timeframe for executing the purchase agreement.
- Specifics on any requirements for continuing employment of the franchisee, consulting on the part of the franchisee or covenants not-to-compete.
- Contingencies including franchisor approval and the successful acquisition of any required permits and licenses.

Unfortunately for the seller, the buyer will probably insist that the letter of intent be non-binding pending completion of due diligence and final agreements, although the letter can be binding on confidentiality to protect the seller. In transactions involving a professional specialist, the letter of intent may be replaced by an offer/acceptance form, like those used in real estate property transactions. These typically are binding and subject to cancellation only if contingencies are not met (i.e., a failure to obtain franchisor approval). In these situations, the nature of the contingencies and the timeframe for their completion (due diligence in particular) should be carefully thought through.

The buyer also assesses the strength and consistency of the franchise system by talking with other franchisees.

The process of due diligence begins after the execution of the letter or memorandum. The typical buyer is looking over legal structure, products and services, suppliers and vendors, sales, facilities, employees and personnel policies, financial records, reporting systems, vendor and creditor relations, etc. The buyer also assesses the strength and consistency of the franchise system by talking with other franchisees. The seller might provide names of supportive franchisees who will give a positive view to the prospective buyer. The prospective buyer will also be working with the franchisor, making sure that the franchisor will approve the sale, understanding what protections there are for the territory, learning what items must be purchased from the franchisor and what services and support are provided, finding out what royalties and other performance, training and insurance criteria are required.

These are added elements often found in the final sales document:

1. Representations and warranties will be required both from the seller and buyer. The buyer will make the greater number of requests for warranties, asking the seller to affirm that:
    *   there is proper authority to sell the business and that the legal house is in order;
    *   the contracts and leases of the business are in good standing and not in threat of being terminated;
    *   there aren't any undisclosed litigants;
    *   there aren't any liens or encumbrances on the company's assets;
    *   the financial statements are fair and accurate;
    *   all taxes have been paid; and/or
    *   there are no hidden liabilities withheld from the buyer.

    The sellers, on the other hand, will want assurance that any entity acquiring the franchise business is in good standing, that is, meeting any legal requirements, and that the buyer has the financial resources to execute the sale, among others.

2. Covenants not to compete may also be included in this document or executed separately. Typically, covenants cover a period of three to five years; beyond that, enforceability might be an issue. Also, covenants must be limited to a geographic area.

3. Any outstanding conditions that need to be met may also be included. For instance, the franchisee may have to agree to operate the company without any major harm or damage or material change in the business until the transfer of ownership has occurred on a date set in the future.

4. Indemnification requirements typically aimed at protecting the buyer are also included. Duration of the indemnification may become an issue. Sometimes there is a timeline added to indemnification period and a maximum amount so the seller doesn't have to live with a sword hanging over his/her head. An escrow account may be set up for this purpose, with a written understanding of what can be paid from the escrow account. If, in the past, the franchisee has given personal guarantees to the franchisor and/or landlords, and they cannot be removed, then indemnification requirements are critical; otherwise, the contingency liabilities may come back to haunt the selling franchisee.

5. Issues specific to the franchisee or franchise chain are also addressed in the final sales document.

At this point, the final documents are circulated among signing parties until all the issues and modifications are completed and the magic moment arrives—the time to sign.

> *The ink is dry on the sales document, but until the business has been turned over and payment has been made, the deal is not complete.*

But surprise! . . . Signing the sales document is not the end of the process. The transaction has to close as well. There can be significant delays between execution of the sales document and closing—for a variety of good and not-so-good reasons. This may turn out to be the most nerve-wracking period of all for the selling franchisee. The ink is dry on the sales document, but until the business has been turned over and payment has been made, the deal is not complete. From the selling franchisee's perspective, there is a tremendous advantage in making this period as short as practical. While the buyer may request time to set up bank accounts, legally establish a business entity, organize a management group, clear up other projects before turning full attention to the new business, etc., the seller will want to effect the changeover as soon as possible. This is especially true if there are concerns about a premature leak to employees about the impending sale; hence, this is one area where the selling franchisee may want to hold firm in insisting upon the earliest reasonable date. Unless there are significant reasons for delay, the period should be as short as possible between the signing of the sale document and closing, since in general, delays work to the advantage of the buyer and to the detriment of the seller.

Managing the Transition

The sales document is signed. The new group has taken over the operation. The transaction has closed. Payment has occurred, or at least the initial payment has been received. The franchisee is now *free at last*, or is he/she? There is still a fair amount of work to be accomplished, both regarding issues involving the new owner's transition and in the winding down of the former entity's affairs.

This work typically takes 3 to 12 months, depending on the number of units/properties involved and the complexity of entities and investors involved. There are numerous external parties to notify of the change (vendors, government agencies), services to cancel (insurance, payroll), unanticipated expenses to pay and records to organize and prepare for long-term storage. Funds need to be earmarked for audits which may be triggered by the closing of the business, particularly audits relating to taxes based on sales figures. These items are just suggestive of the items that need attending to in the process of winding down; each company will have a slightly different list.

Not allowing enough time for this final stage deprives the seller of the satisfaction of putting everything in its place.

What is important is that the franchisee allow sufficient time for the *winding down* and *letting go* process, rather than rushing into some other activity. This is the last stage of the sales process and tends to be dismissed as simple mechanics. The nature of the work, following through on dozens of mindless and incredibly boring details, belies its importance. Moreover, not allowing enough time for this final stage deprives the seller of the satisfaction of putting everything in its place. Finishing the job thoroughly and completely creates a sense of completion which allows the franchisee to move more gracefully into the next phase of his/her work life.

With regard to the transition internally within the company, the franchisee needs to have a well-orchestrated plan for the transfer of the business. The transition process needs to be jointly worked out between the franchisee and buyer so that it meets the needs of both parties. A list of what needs to be done, when and by whom can be circulated between the seller and buyer to make sure that all bases are covered.

The most immediate items to plan and execute involve the announcement of the change in ownership to employees, in what order (as a courtesy, managers and supervisors are told first), how employees' urgent concerns and questions will be answered and who will make the announcements and when. If the transfer of ownership involves two different companies (as opposed to the sale of stock, for example), then arrangements also need to be made for final pay (vacation, bonuses, commissions, etc.) as well as repayment of any outstanding employee advances. The selling franchisee may also want to request that employees sign a letter of resignation from their former company in order to avoid future claims.

Predictably enough, employee concerns involve assurance of continuity in their own daily activities (what they will be doing and who their supervisor is) and assurance that their pay and benefits will remain unchanged, or if they are going to change, what the new compensation will be. The selling franchisee needs to be meticulous in arranging for the transfer of medical and dental benefits so that there is no period of time that is uncovered. The termination of the selling franchisee's benefit program needs to coincide with the start-up of the new employer's program. COBRA notifications may or may not be required, depending on the change in status of employees and whether or not any employees are deemed ineligible by the new employer's benefit program. Insurance providers can help with these kinds of questions.

For supervisors, it is critical to get answers on practical questions—who is in charge, when will they meet the new owners, who should have keys or security access to the business, what are the new bank accounts, what is the organizational structure, what changes can be expected, what are the names of the new owners, etc. To the extent that both the franchisee and buyer can anticipate the issues that will surface, the transition can be made that much smoother.

> *It is easy to underestimate the emotional impact*
> *of turning over a business to another party.*

In the event the franchisee is going to continue to work in the business for a period of time, it is critical that he/she adopts the new owner's philosophy and approach. That may be easier said than done. It is easy to underestimate the emotional impact of turning over a business to another party, especially after having brought it into existence and developing it for a period of years. For the franchisee who will abruptly end his/her work in the business, saying "good-bye" will probably not be an easy thing to do or a happy occasion—even when the sale was eagerly awaited. In fact, it is not uncommon for both former employees and the selling franchisee to grieve over the loss of familiar ties and routines. The seller may also feel guilty about abandoning ship. Many emotions—relief, sadness, guilt, exhilaration, fatigue, joy, regrets—may be experienced. It is also understandable—if irrational—for the selling franchisee to have a considerable emotional investment in the success of the business long after it has been sold.

A large part of the franchisee's identity may be tied up with being the owner, and without that identity the person may feel lost.

As we said at the beginning, letting go of an organization which the franchisee has devoted many years of his/her life in building is a major life event and should not be underestimated. A large part of the franchisee's identity may be tied up with being the owner, and without that identity the person may feel lost. This emotional experience is somewhat equivalent to the *empty nest* syndrome some parents feel when their offspring leave home. In fact, it may be tempting to interfere and criticize how the new management is operating the business as a way of denying that the business has changed hands. Such efforts are counterproductive and need to be abandoned as soon as the impulse to interfere occurs. Like a young person who needs to leave home to grow into a responsible adult, the selling franchisee needs to let the business go so it can become what the new ownership intends it to be—whether better, worse or something else entirely.

While the *letting go* process is working itself out, the selling franchisee still has to attend to all of the issues involved in *winding down* the business. For a multi-unit operation, the corporate or business office needs to be closed. By now, the business office employees have been told what is going to occur. Layoffs or out-placement processes should be underway. The franchisee may want to give a bonus to one or more critical employees, to be paid only if they stay employed until the end of the process, thereby assuring continuity.

Typically, the *winding down* also involves legally dissolving the entity; filing final tax returns, notifying utility companies, canceling service contracts and insurance, notifying government and tax authorities, resolving any outstanding invoices or liabilities, paying outstanding taxes, arranging for the storage of records, answering questions and getting information to the new owners and setting up provisions for future expenses. The *winding down* work trickles away over time, taking less and less attention each week, until one day there is no more work to do.

> *Remember the old adage, "Act in haste and repent in leisure."*

When the last piece of work is finally done, the former franchisee may sigh, take a deep breath, then schedule a well-deserved rest. It may be tempting to jump immediately into something new and demanding to fill the void, but a more prudent approach might be to invest any money resulting from the sale, sit back and take some time for reflection. The franchisee has just suffered through or enjoyed a major life event—a kind of *work divorce*. Just as one would advise a newly divorced person to wait a few months before jumping back into marriage, it might also be prudent for the selling franchisee to take an equivalent breather—six months at a minimum.

The old adage, "Act in haste and repent in leisure" definitely applies in this situation. For most people, operating a franchise is a demanding task requiring intense focus. Rather than rushing into another compelling job requiring major effort, it might be a better use of time to look up and around, see what's been happening in the world while the nose was to the grindstone, smell the roses and celebrate. After all, this franchisee is finally *free at last*.

Legal Implications of the Sale of an Existing Franchise

Generally, the sale of a franchise is a business decision. That business decision, however, has numerous implications for a minimum of three parties—the transferor franchisee, the transferee and the franchisor. In addition, other players, such as bankers, equipment lessors, real property lessors and business and real estate brokers have a stake in the transaction. Just the prospect of a sale may trigger legal obligations and rights within the franchise relationship which cannot be overlooked, lest the franchise agreement could be violated at a most inopportune time.

THE FRANCHISEE: WHAT TO EXPECT AND WHAT TO AVOID

First, the legal house must be put in order. The franchisee contemplating a franchise sale must begin to review various legal documents to determine the steps which must be taken at various stages of the process. The most important legal document, and the one which is the actual subject of the transfer, is the franchise agreement.

Franchise Agreement Issues and Concerns

Although the best time to deal with unconscionable provisions is when negotiating the franchise agreement, a good relationship with the franchisor can go a long way toward obtaining approval for a transfer.

The Ubiquitous Transfer Provision: It is common to find a transfer provision that includes the right of franchisor approval before a transfer can occur. It is also common to discover language that states the transfer will not be unreasonably withheld. What is somewhat out of the ordinary is the transfer provision which states the franchisor has sole discretion in approving the transferee, or that approval may be unreasonably withheld, or withheld for any reason. Should a franchisee encounter this restrictive language, the sales process could get bogged down by unjustified rejection of prospects. Although the best time to deal with unconscionable provisions is when negotiating the franchise agreement, a good relationship with the franchisor can go a long way toward obtaining approval for a transfer, especially when faced with an unreasonable provision.

The Right of First Refusal: Provided the franchise agreement does not contain an unreasonable right to withhold approval, the next major hurdle is the franchisor's right of first refusal. Many franchise agreements include that provision, even if the franchisor never purchased, or has no intention of buying back, a franchise. Basically, this is a notice provision, alerting the franchisor to the fact that you have received an offer for the franchised business. Depending on the period of time the franchisor has to make a decision on purchasing the franchise, the delay could have a chilling effect on the sales process. This is especially true if the franchisor is one known for repurchasing franchises.

The right of first refusal generally requires the franchisee to submit the exact offer received from the purchaser, in order for the franchisor and the prospective purchaser to be in the same purchasing position. Here again, timing is key. If the franchisor does not want to accept the offer, but the franchisee is unable to complete the sale with his/her buyer within the given time period in the franchise agreement, the franchisor will once again have the opportunity to purchase the franchise under a new right of first refusal. As mentioned earlier, a franchisee may consider asking for a *first right to offer* instead of a first right of refusal.

Many franchisors will allow franchisees to ask them up front to waive their first refusal rights for a sale they are negotiating. A franchisee should ask if their franchisor would, too! If the franchisor will agree to that, the sale will be much easier to negotiate, finance and close, and much faster to conclude.

Up-front Transfer Fees: Some franchise agreements will require that a transfer fee be paid when an offer is submitted to the franchisor and the fee is refundable in full, or in large part, if the sale does not close. This is clearly an unnecessary burden placed on the franchisee, who will not have use of the prospective purchaser's money until the closing of the transaction. A variation of this condition is to require the prospective purchaser to submit a substantial down payment, to be held in escrow, with the offer. Although this requirement discourages certain purchasers, it may in fact help weed out the tire kickers and information seekers.

Assignment or New Agreement: The transfer provision must be consulted to determine exactly what the transferor franchisee is granted the right to sell. The knee-jerk answer is, "My franchise, of course." Often, this is not the case. There are at least three possibilities. First, the knee-jerk answer; in certain cases, the transferor can, in fact, sell or assign the agreement the franchisee has lived with for all these years. This is especially true in cases where older franchise agreements with franchisors whose attorneys did not slip in abhorrent *then current* language. In these cases, the franchisee knows what there is to sell, and the seller will not have to be concerned with the franchisor's registration or updating of its offering circular, since the sale will be for the account of the franchisee. (See *Drake v. Maid-Rite Co.*, CCH Business Franchise Guide Ind. App. 11,199 1997. The sale of a franchise by a franchisee for his own account was specifically exempted from the statute's disclosure requirements.) The documentation involved in this type of sale may consist only of an assignment agreement. Nevertheless, the franchisee's attorney should insist on a complete break, with his/her client having no further obligation to the franchisor.

The second possibility also allows the sale of a franchise or, in this case, a franchise's assets but not a franchise agreement. Why? The reason relates to the language in the transfer provision of the franchise agreement which states that the transferee will sign the *then-current agreement* being offered to new prospects at the time of sale. On the surface, this may seem fair to the rest of the new prospects, but closer scrutiny raises some difficult issues.

First, and foremost, the selling franchisee did not operate under this new agreement. Moreover, he/she may not have even read it since there was no reason to possess it. All of a sudden, the selling franchisee finds him/herself on the defensive.

Since the franchise agreement transfer provision cannot be changed at the time of sale, franchisees must protect themselves as much as possible from post-closing claims.

Since the operation was based on a six percent royalty and one percent advertising, and net profits reflect income using those unshakable figures, the business will take on a whole new look with an eight percent royalty, a two percent advertising fund and a variety of other new requirements. The issue also touches on disclosure—the franchisee's, not the franchisor's. It is incumbent on the selling franchisee to make it clear to the purchaser that he/she may be buying your business but will operate it under a different set of rules. Consequently, financial disclosures must include a caveat to prevent this purchaser from coming back with a fraudulent inducement claim. Since the franchise agreement transfer provision cannot be changed at the time of sale, franchisees must protect themselves as much as possible from post-closing claims.

> *The longer one owns a franchise, the more likely the then-current franchise agreement may differ.*

The other issue raised is the ability to promote an unfamiliar agreement. Whereas a franchisee knows and understands the business, thanks to a franchisor's drafting, the franchisee will not be able to fully represent that, it is in fact, his/her business for sale. What a franchisee can *sell* will be different, and usually less valuable, than what a franchisee *owns*. This is a difficult concept to grasp. Nevertheless, the longer one owns a franchise, the more likely the then-current franchise agreement may differ.

The only positive trade-off for the buyer is that a *new* franchise usually will have a *new* and full term ahead of it, while on assignment of the seller's *old* franchise will only be good for its unexpired term. At the end of the unexpired term the buyer would face renewal into the unknown *then current* new franchise.

The third possibility is a hybrid and creates a new set of issues for the seller. This hybrid results when the transfer provision language is ambiguous or may actually give the franchisor the right to choose which agreement to use. The question then is, which one is sold? In theory, the franchisee would like to sell his/her agreement, for the reasons already noted. Yet, the franchisor may opt for the new agreement, which brings him/her more benefit. This perplexity can have a negative effect on the sale. To address this issue, a franchisee should approach his/her franchisor imminent to the sale to ascertain which product or service is being sold. Again, the franchisee's attorney should insist on the sale of the existing agreement. If successful, the franchisee will have a clear advantage.

Updating: Factored into many transfer provisions is the requirement that the selling franchisee will bring the franchised premises up to the then-current standards. As a selling franchisee, this provision must be clearly understood, as it could delay or prevent the sale. The issues presented by this requirement are both legal and business-related since they involve franchisee obligations as well as economics. If approval of the transfer is based on refurbishing, remodeling and redecorating, this must be considered in setting the selling price, and/or must be made a purchaser's obligation. The selling franchisee receives nothing from the upgrades once he/she leaves the franchise. For this reason, the burden for making those payments must be shifted to the incoming franchisee.

Certain franchise agreements actually restrict upgrading in the last year of the term. This raises the question of whether the franchisee who sells in the last year of the term would be required to do any upgrading. Arguably, the franchisor can look to the incoming franchisee, since renewal of the franchise agreement will take place within the year. But, can the franchisor impose the obligation on the selling franchisee? This question really asks whether one provision of the franchise agreement takes precedence over another. It's a question worthy of a franchisee's consideration.

Default: As noted earlier, the transfer provision in the franchise agreement controls the sale and lists the requirements which must be met to complete the sale. One of those requirements is often the good standing of the franchisee. Franchisors reserve the right to withhold approval if a franchisee is in default under the franchise agreement. Many transfers do, however, take place when the transferor franchisee is in default.

Defaults occur when the franchisee stops paying royalties and/or advertising/marketing fees.

Generally, defaults occur when the franchisee stops paying royalties and/or advertising/marketing fees. This amounts to owing the franchisor money. When a monetary default exists and a franchisee desires to sell the franchise, franchisors will sometimes not stand in the way of the sale, provided the debt to the franchisor can be satisfied from the closing. From the franchisor's standpoint, this is a good way to get rid of a problem. From the franchisee's standpoint, this is a good way to clear debt and exit the franchise. Both parties win. If the default is non-monetary, the selling franchisee may be required to cure the default before the sale can occur.

Default of the franchise agreement at any time is very serious.

This chapter is neither suggesting that a defaulting franchisee can coast to the closing by curing the default at the last possible moment nor that default at the time of closing is different than at any other time. Default of the franchise agreement at any time is very serious. Default at or around the time of transfer may prevent or delay closing. A delay in closing due to the actions of the selling franchisee, which leads to a *notice of default,* may also be a breach of the asset purchase agreement and could jeopardize franchisor approval or actually kill the sale. Some franchisors look for ways to get a franchisee who is in default, and some others are happy to have a franchisee who is in default sell out and go away.

Franchisees must also be aware of any cross-default conditions. A cross-default occurs when one of a number of agreements are breached. The breach of one could be the catalyst to terminate another. Therefore, failure to pay rent could not only cause a default in a lease but could serve as a reason for default under the franchise agreement, although other provisions of the franchise agreement have been upheld.

General Release: A common exit document used by franchisors at the time of transfer is the general release. Through one signature, a franchisee can release the franchisor, its shareholders, officers, directors, employees, agents, representatives, attorneys and affiliates and forever forego the right to file any claim against the franchisor for any breach of contract, economic discrimination, unfair franchise practice, antitrust or disclosure violations, etc. Not surprisingly, the franchisor does not release its claims, if any, against the franchisee, unless mutual general releases are signed. Mutual general releases are a rarity if not negotiated when the franchise is purchased.

The one-sided general release should be avoided at all costs.

If possible, the one-sided general release should be avoided at all costs. It is an unfair, forced expression which releases the franchisor from all claims—whether legitimate or not. Except for approving the transfer (which the franchisor should not have the right to block without good reason) there is no good reason for this unilateral absolution. If, on the other hand, the relationship has been a pleasant one, the franchisor hasn't committed a breach nor violated state laws, the release will be of no practical consequence. Whether a franchisee can be required to sign a general release at all is the subject of much debate and litigation. Since the general release is a contract provision, it is difficult to get around-except in states where it is not permitted in franchise contracts.

The Lease

After the franchise agreement, the most important document to review is the lease. Leases do not have transfer provisions. Instead, they have *assignment* and *sublet* provisions. The discretion as to whether to approve a new lessee lies with the lessor. The lease is important for obvious reasons. The seller has operated the business from a specific location. If the purchaser would not be able to continue at the current leased premises, the expense of moving the business may not warrant buying it.

Since maintaining the same location has definite advantages, agreements to purchase are often contingent on the purchaser obtaining the same, or equally favorable, lease. Provided the prospective franchisee is able to obtain a new lease—not simply an assignment—the selling franchisee's attorney should do whatever possible to remove the seller's name and any personal guarantees made from the lease. This is also true for an assignment, but it is much more difficult since lessors are reluctant to release anyone they can look to for rent. But much will depend on timing. Lessors may be more likely to grant an assignment with no strings attached late in the lease.

Sublease: Certain large franchisors have opted to become prime lessee for a number of reasons. These include reserving a good site before a franchisee is identified, being the only acceptable tenant for a landlord due to the franchisor's net worth, maintaining the lease as a control mechanism; and others. In any case, the franchisee becomes a sublessee and does not enter into a contract directly with the lessor, but instead contracts with the franchisor.

There are positives and negatives to this approach, but suffice it to say a selling franchisee has yet one more hurdle to overcome when positioned as a sublessee. Added to the normal qualification process of the lessor-lessee is the sublessor-sublessee procedure. Both the lessor and the sub-lessor will undoubtedly become involved with such matters as security, rent increases, administrative and promotional fees, percentage rent, remodeling and a host of other items which can be time consuming and expensive and may delay the sale.

If the selling franchisee is a sublessee, a request should be made to the franchisor far in advance of the closing date to determine what will be required, the timeframe involved and the procedure for obtaining a full release from the franchisor related to the sublease.

Other Contracts

Throughout the time the seller has owned the franchise, other contracts may have been executed, such as equipment leases, security agreements, financing contracts and mortgages, advertising contracts, employment agreements, etc. For those contracts which remain in force at the time of the sale, the selling franchisee must either terminate them or assign them to the purchaser. Notice must be given to service providers, and ample time must be allowed for background checks and legal approvals. Many require the consent of the other party. The seller should have a complete list of these contracts before the sale takes place. Once the seller understands which contracts are involved, action should be taken to either terminate or assign them with no resulting liability.

> *Franchisors favor the use of the general release to limit their liability going forward.*

Termination Agreement

The sale of a franchise triggers an exit procedure which generally involves a termination agreement. As noted, franchisors favor the use of the general release to limit their liability going forward. It is not uncommon to also be handed a termination agreement which terminates the franchise agreement with the seller on the date of sale. The purpose of the termination agreement is obvious, however, the effect for the seller is very important, since no further obligations can accrue to the seller from that day forward. The termination agreement is more a matter of record keeping and not a document to avoid or heavily negotiate—unless it includes general release language not required by the franchise agreement.

Corporation Approval of the Sale

If the seller is a corporation, there is a small legal checklist to bear in mind. Most purchasers and franchisors will request a *certificate of good standing.* This is a simple matter provided the corporation has filed its annual report and paid the nominal fees to maintain its existence. As the date for closing approaches, the seller's attorney should prepare a detailed corporate resolution for execution by the board of directors. This resolution provides details concerning transfer of the franchise agreement, the lease, other contracts, the assumed corporate name and any other tangible and intangible property, including good will.

If the stock bears a legend stating that the sale or transfer is subject to the franchise agreement, the legend should be removed after the closing takes place. Likewise, if the purpose clause of the articles of incorporation is specific to the business of the franchise, it should be changed and the franchise-specific language should be replaced with a purpose clause giving the corporation the right to conduct all business lawful under the corporation act in the state where the corporation was incorporated.

All assumed corporate names should be canceled as of the date of closing. Since many franchisees apply for and receive an assumed name registration using the franchisor's trade name, the seller should coordinate with the buyer the cancellation of the seller's registration and the buyer's application to adopt the same name. This provides for continuity.

THE FRANCHISOR'S ROLE

The franchisor's role runs the gamut from being very limited to becoming very involved. This is, in part, a function of the terms of the franchise agreement, the type of buyer and the interest in the sale. This section has already discussed the franchisor's role created by the requirements of the transfer provision. What follows are additional or related requirements.

Offering Circulars

> *If "the then current franchise agreement" is the only choice, the franchisor must be legally bound to provide its current franchise offering circular to the buyer.*

If *"the then current franchise agreement"* is the only choice, the franchisor must be legally bound to provide its current franchise offering circular to the buyer. In registration states, this means the franchisor will have to maintain its registration. In filing and notice sales, those with lesser requirements, the franchisor must still make sure it is legally permitted to continue to sell franchises. In this regard, a resale is tantamount to a sale, since the franchisor will offer the then-current agreement, disclose the current offering circular and execute only the then-current agreement. Due to this legal requirement, a buyer will be unable to sign the franchise agreement for a minimum of 10 business days after receiving the franchise offering circular. This scenario does not allow for an assignment by the seller, since the seller never had a contractual right to make an assignment.

Franchisor Approval

The entire sale hinges on whether the franchisor ultimately approves the buyer. Even if a franchisor chooses not to approve one or more buyers, the franchisor is not considered as legally playing an integral role in the franchise sale. With or without providing disclosure, the franchisor can impact the sale, sometimes in a very negative manner. The approval decision can be made at various points throughout the process. For example, the franchisor could reject a buyer who may be a competitor. The franchisor could reject a buyer for lack of financial wherewithal to meet the challenges of the franchise system. Or the franchisor can reject a buyer for failure to satisfactorily complete training.

In a California case featured in the March 20, 1998 *Business Franchise Guide,* Judge Levi of the U.S. District Court for the Eastern District of California found "that the UFOC and License Agreement do disclose the fact that satisfactory completion of the applicant training program is a factor considered in approving sales or assignments of franchise interests and that no sale or transfer to others is permitted without McDonald's advance written approval." The training provision was upheld. Although four potential purchasers were rejected for failure to meet training standards, the plaintiff could not convince the court that McDonald's committed fraud, however, the court found an unfair practice may have been committed. (*Perez v. McDonald's Corp.* CCH BUSINESS FRANCHISE GUIDE D.C. CA. 11,329 1998)

The seller has little, if any, control to change the result of any of these situations. Consequently, selling a franchise is no foregone conclusion even if a contract is tendered by a would-be, seemingly-qualified buyer.

Franchisor-Imposed Obligations

Once past the hurdle of the qualifications process, and provided the franchisor does not reserve its rights to reject the buyer all the way up to the closing, the seller will be faced with transfer obligations imposed by the franchise agreement. Sellers are required to bring all accounts with the franchisor, and sometimes the franchisor's affiliates, current. This means the seller must calculate royalty and advertising up to the date of closing. Where practical, closings take place at franchisor's offices or in the presence of a franchisor representative. This is done so the franchisor can be assured all necessary documents are signed and all monies owed are paid before completely approving the transfer.

Although less involved than the seller, the limited role the franchisor plays is very important. At various stages, the franchisor can bring the entire process to a halt—either by exercising a right of first refusal, rejecting a buyer for any number of valid reasons or issuing a valid default and termination notice. The franchisor also has a stake in shepherding the process smoothly to allow for a transition from one franchisee to the next so that there is little, if any, interruption in the business. As noted previously, a good relationship with the franchisor can go a long way.

THE PURCHASE AGREEMENT

The document used to coordinate all transfer of tangible and intangible property, recite all consideration, set forth all representations and warranties, provide for indemnification and non-competition and require the various approvals is the *purchase agreement*. Although no rule of thumb exists, the buyer's attorney will normally take the responsibility to draft this document since the buyer requires much greater protection than the seller. The importance of this document cannot be overstated, since it acts as a blueprint for the entire sales process. So selling franchisees are cautioned to examine this document with great care and have accountants and attorneys examine and make any necessary changes to the document before signing.

Conclusion

The sale of a franchise and the legal implications attendant thereto cannot be separated. The very decision to sell is reason enough to begin to put the legal house in order. Understanding the franchise agreement, the leases involved, the third party contracts related to the business and the applicable disclosure laws are all necessary to enable the sales effort to proceed. After all, the objective is to sell the franchise and be free of its obligations. Anything to help foster that objective will benefit the selling franchisee and those working with him/her.

And, needless to say, it is always a good investment to find a good business lawyer who is also well experienced in franchise transactions to guide you along. The help of a good accountant is also extremely valuable.

CHAPTER V
FRANCHISE BUSINESS LAW

Basics of Contract Law, Employment Law and Leases

In addition to the obligations and requirements contracted by and between a franchisee and its franchisor according to the franchise/license agreement, a franchisee must also concern him/herself with basic business and real estate issues. Typical in most franchise agreements, the franchisee is exclusively responsible for day-to-day operations. Failure to properly attend to basic business practices in the operation of the franchise can be as detrimental as being in breach of one's franchise agreement. Following is a brief overview of several business concepts every franchisee should review—either before going into the franchise relationship or during the operation of the business—to ensure operations function with practices best suited for a particular franchise and its owners. Keep in mind that each issue might be used as a starting point for discussion with a franchise attorney or accountant.

Type of Entity

> *The type of business entity may not isolate or protect an individual franchisee from the franchisor, but it will have benefits to third parties, such as one's customers, vendors, landlord, etc.*

The type of entity selected for the business operation can have a dramatic effect on the liability of the individual franchisee. Some franchise systems do not allow a corporation, limited liability company, limited partnership or general partnership to sign a franchise agreement. If the system does allow it, it typically requires all principals of such an entity to sign personal guarantees. Therefore, the type of entity may not necessarily isolate or protect an individual franchisee from the franchisor, but it will have benefits to third parties, such as one's customers, vendors, landlord, etc.

Even though an individual may be signing the franchise agreement, the agreement may contain a provision allowing for its assignment or assignment of the operations of the franchise system to an entity such as a corporation, limited liability company, limited partnership or general partnership.

The benefit of having an entity other than the individual franchisee operate the day-to-day operations of the franchise is that the responsibilities and potential liabilities are transferred to a non-personal entity. For example, Mr. Patel can sign a franchise agreement, but ABC Corporation actually operates the day-to-day franchise business. In such a situation, should a third party, such as a guest, slip and fall on ABC Corporation's franchise premises, the injured party would then have a claim against ABC Corporation, not the principal, Mr. Patel. Accordingly, should the injured party be successful in obtaining a judgment, then the party could only seek payment on the judgment from the corporation, not the individual. For example, if Don Jones obtains a $100,000,000 judgment against ABC Corporation, and ABC Corporation only has $10,000 in assets, that could be the extent of Don Jones' recovery (except in the event of insurance coverage or a rare exception to the general rule). The same scenario would be true under the format of a limited liability company, professional corporation or limited partnership. A general partnership, however, may bring personal liability to each of the individual partners.

The following is a brief description of the available entities:

Sole Proprietorship: A sole proprietorship is one in which the individual franchisee retains and performs the day-to-day duties and operation, incurring any and all liabilities. A new entity is not created to operate the franchise business.

Partnership: This is a grouping of two or more individuals who, in their individual capacities, contract with one another to create a partnership to operate the franchise business. A partnership offers certain possible tax advantages, but partners may be subject to unlimited personal liability, and the partnership entity is not typically recommended to protect against personal liability.

Limited Partnership: A limited partnership is one in which there is a general partner and group of limited partners. The general partner maintains most, if not all, management authority, responsibility and liability in connection with the operation of the limited partnership's business. The *investors* (limited partners) have no management authority or rights. In order to create the most effective limited partnership with respect to liability issues, the general partner should be a corporation rather than an individual. If a limited partner should somehow obtain management and/or authority for the operation of the limited partnership, he/she could then be subject to personal liability.

Corporation: A corporation is an entity created pursuant to state law. For example, a corporation created in Texas is a *Texas corporation.* That corporation may then do business in other states as long as it is duly registered in each and every state in which it does business. This is sometimes referred to as a "foreign" corporation (i.e. a Texas corporation doing business in California). A corporation ordinarily provides the individual shareholders with limited liability. Therefore, should the corporate entity be found responsible for some form of breach or injury, the injured parties could only seek retribution from the corporate entity, not the individual shareholders (barring certain rare exceptions)

There are many advantages to a C corporation versus an S corporation but they must be reviewed on a case by case basis.

In the formation of a corporation, there are various tax determinations to be made. The most common choice is whether to incorporate as a C or an S corporation. The C and S refer to specific subchapters of the Internal Revenue Code. Typically, an S-corporation is for closely-held corporations which do not foresee going public in the very near future. It allows for profits and losses to flow directly from the corporation to the individual shareholders without *double* taxation. A C-corporation, on the other hand, retains all its profits and liabilities at the corporate level, then disburses such items as deemed feasible to its individual shareholders and is taxed at both the corporate and shareholder levels. There are many advantages to a C-corporation versus an S-corporation, but these must be reviewed on a case-by-case basis with lawyers and accountants. As far as liability is concerned, there is no difference between a C-corporation and an S-corporation.

As already noted, a corporation is a creature of state law, and therefore, it may be advantageous to incorporate in one state over another. Certain states have laws that are more advantageous to a corporation and its shareholders from a number of standpoints—operations, tax considerations, take-over aspects, etc. At one time, many believed Delaware was *the* state in which to incorporate, since it had the most progressive corporate laws. Today, however, a number of states have implemented statutes similar to Delaware.

Limited Liability Company: A limited liability company (LLC) is a relatively new concept, which is also created pursuant to state law. An LLC is a hybrid which may now give one the benefit of both a corporation and partnership. An LLC also has more flexibility as to the allocation of profits and losses versus that of a corporation, particularly an S-corporation.

An LLC is of significant benefit to those involved in owning real estate.

The use of the LLC is changing on a daily basis, as it is a relatively new entity with relevant bodies of law being developed and relevant state laws being modified. An LLC is of significant benefit to those involved in owning real estate. There can be virtually no personal liability for individual principals, compared to a corporation where there is the possibility, however rare, that one could pierce the corporate veil and claim personal liability on the part of individual shareholders.

Professional Corporation: A professional corporation is similar to a *regular* corporation but is limited to *professionals* such as doctors, lawyers, accountants, architects, dentists, chiropractors, etc. A professional corporate entity is one which allows for the incorporation of a professional so he/she may take advantage of various tax strategies and limited liability in dealings of his/her business (i.e. vendors, landlords, etc). As a matter of public policy, a professional cannot waive his/her personal liability to his/her client. For example, a doctor cannot hide behind a corporate shield in the event that he/she commits malpractice.

Relationship of Business Entity with Franchise

Relationship with the Franchisor. As noted previously the franchisor typically requires an individual (and in many circumstances, the individual's spouse) to personally sign the franchise agreement and, through provisions of the franchise agreement, allows the individual to transfer the rights, if not the entire agreement, to an operating entity such as a corporation, limited liability, limited partnership, etc. However, in the transfer or assignment of the franchise agreement to the new entity, the franchisor will typically require a personal guarantee to be signed by the individual franchisees and also require certain restrictions as to the ownership interest of the entity created for the operation of the franchised business. This may possibly be negotiated with the franchisor. The franchisee should try to limit individuals signing to either the husband *or* the wife in order to protect marital assets. It is also highly recommended, though rarely accepted, to have only the entity sign the franchise agreement and to do so without personal guarantees.

Relationship with Customers, Clients, Vendors and Other Third Parties. Once an entity has been created for the purpose of operating the franchise, it is imperative that the entity be known to all third parties. This way, any claim is brought against the operating entity, not the individual. In other words, if a corporation is created and Mike Patel is the president, he will need to make sure that when signing contracts, letters or representing himself to the public that he identifies himself as an *employee* of the corporation. Otherwise, if the entity is not known to a vendor, customer or third party, there has never been an effort to disclose the operating entity and the only association and contract they have is with a specific individual, Mike Patel could be subject to personal liability.

In many franchise agreements, the franchisor requires the franchisees to identify themselves with a plaque at the franchise location that states *Independently owned and operated by ABC, Inc.* This benefits the franchisor by placing the public on notice that the franchisor is not serving as owner and operator of the facility. It also is a benefit to the franchisee who identifies the existence of the operating entity and the individual.

Insurance

It is imperative to have comprehensive insurance to cover as many situations as a franchisee can reasonably afford.

Depending on the type of franchise and the letter of the agreement, there are various insurance requirements. It is important to review the franchise agreement insurance requirements with an insurance agent prior to signing. A prospective franchisee must determine whether he/she can fulfill the requirements, and most importantly, afford the cost of the insurance. Also, it is imperative that a franchisee have comprehensive insurance that would cover as many possible situations as he/she can reasonably afford. Insurance requirements include fire and casualty insurance, general liability insurance, auto insurance, business interruption insurance, errors and omissions, products liability, worker's compensation insurance, etc.

Internal Documentation/Controls

After deciding which type of entity with which to operate a franchise, there are certain agreements and other documentation necessary to provide for the internal operation and ownership of the selected entity.

Sole Proprietorship: As a sole proprietor, there is no additional documentation required since a sole proprietorship is just that—one individual acting in his or her individual capacity. Therefore, the individual is solely responsible for the control and responsibility of the business, including any and all liabilities.

Partnership: A partnership is the joining of two or more individuals as partners. A partnership is typically operated through terms of a partnership agreement which provides for the details as to management, capital investment, working arrangement, voluntary or involuntary dissolution, death of a partner, disability of a partner, termination of the partnership, etc. A partnership agreement is a contract between individual partners. The partnership may be either a general partnership or a limited partnership. Again, as noted previously the general partner is the one who will retain personal liability unless a general corporate partner is utilized. The limited partners, who do not and should not have any management duties or authority, will be limited as to their liability according to their investment in the entity. Also keep in mind that various states require a partnership, in particular a limited partnership, to register with the state in which it is organized.

A corporation is created by virtue of state law and is governed by articles of incorporation and by-laws.

Corporation: A corporation is created by virtue of state law and is governed by articles of incorporation and by-laws. In addition, individual shareholders should enter into what is known as a *shareholders' agreement*, which is similar to a partnership agreement. It provides for the agreed-upon terms as to management, duties, capital investment, death of a shareholder, disability of a shareholder, involuntary and voluntary dissolution, exit strategies, etc. The shareholders' agreement, like the partnership agreement, is an important aspect in the formation of the entity with more than one principal, since it will provide for agreed-upon terms in specific situations. The corporation and partnership can exist without these documents, but they are recommended, since any dispute would then be left to the courts or state statutes, rules or regulations which may be contrary to the desires or benefits of the individual parties.

LLC: Under the format of a limited liability company, there is typically an operating agreement. This agreement is also similar to that of a partnership and shareholders' agreement. It likewise contains provisions as to the internal management and operation of the LLC, including agreed-upon provisions regarding death, disability, involuntary or voluntary termination, managerial duties, etc. In addition, the LLC is similar to a corporation in that there is typically a certificate of organization that needs to be filed with the appropriate office of the state in which it is organized—analogous to a corporation's articles of incorporation.

State laws and case law have provided that, if corporate formalities are not upheld, individual shareholders could be exposed to personal liability.

Additional Corporate Formalities: In order to comply with requirements of a corporate entity, and to maintain limited liability for the corporation's shareholder, it is required that the corporation maintain certain corporate formalities such as minutes, election of officers and directors, fictitious name registration, separate and distinct bank accounts under the name and federal identification number of the corporation and other related matters. There are more formalities required of a corporation than that of an LLC, partnership or sole proprietorship. State laws and case law have provided that, if corporate formalities are not upheld, individual shareholders could be exposed to personal liability. Therefore, it is very important that a corporation maintain its corporate formalities, as tedious as they may be, in order to achieve the true benefits of selecting a corporation as the operating entity.

LEASE ISSUES

Introduction to Leasing in Franchising

In many franchising situations, especially those which utilize store front outlets and office space, the importance of the lease contract can not be overemphasized. After the franchise agreement itself, the lease or sublease, is arguably the most important agreement you will negotiate and sign. Unlike an independent business leasing space, the lease for a franchise outlet may have further restrictions imposed by the franchisor. This complicates the leasing process by adding more requirements and, frequently, an additional approval.

The following will summarize the basics of leasing, the provisions for which franchisees should strenuously negotiate, language to eliminate and certain rights and obligations of the parties.

Favorable Drafting

Similar to franchise agreements, leases are written in favor of the drafter, or the lessor. It is the franchisee's attorney's task to negotiate removal of some of the restrictions and impediments generally found in leases, thus making the lease more acceptable to the franchisee. Setting forth proposed changes in an addendum is one way to alert the lessor. Frequently, making changes directly on the lease and returning the marked-up lease is also an acceptable method for recommending that the lease be modified.

Leasing Basics

The basics of the leasing relationship are not complicated. A lessor offers space for the payment of rent and other *additional rental* items, which may include common area maintenance (CAM), general real estate taxes and insurance. Although highly discouraged, percentage rent is another item which falls into the category of additional rent. Percentage rent is triggered when the lessee crosses a certain revenue barrier. Once this occurs, a calculation is made to determine the amount of rent owed the lessor above base rent. The base rent is normally a function of the amount of leased square feet multiplied by a dollar amount—which represents the going rate or fair market value per square foot. The base rent can be the same throughout the lease or can vary each year, increasing slightly (approximately 2-4 percent) based on some popular barometer such as the Consumer Price Index. The CAM payment and the real estate taxes can also be expected to fluctuate, more often than not increasing each year. Consequently, the monthly checks the lessee writes at the end of the lease may be much different, normally higher, than those checks written at the beginning. Some lessors will quote a single monthly cost, which takes into consideration the base rent, CAM, insurance and real estate taxes.

Rights of the Parties

Subject to the lease, the lessee has the right to quiet enjoyment in the space for its rented purpose. This means that the lessor agrees to comply with terms of the contract. Further, the lessor agrees to undertake certain obligations, which may mean any number of things such as:

- Making repairs the lessor has agreed to make;
- Providing services contracted for;
- Refraining from leasing to competitors or creating competition within the shopping area;
- Giving notice of defaults and providing cure periods and/or
- Replacing the roof if contracted to do so.

Subject to the lease, the lessor also has rights and expectations that the lessee will undertake certain obligations. The lessor has the right to expect that the rent is paid timely, including additional rent and percentage rent, if negotiated. The lessor has the right to look to the lessee to maintain and repair that which is within the premises and expect the lessee to conform to the rules and regulations attached to the lease. The lessor also has the right to approve signage. If the lessee defaults, the lessor has the right to terminate the lease and impose various remedies to collect rent and other amounts due after termination.

Lease vs. Sublease

By reviewing the master lease, the franchisee will be able to determine the amount of rent the lease requires.

The signatories to a lease may be the franchisor and the lessor, in which case the franchisee becomes a sublessee. In order to control the location, a direct lease between the franchisee and the lessor is preferable and will give the franchisee more options. If the franchisee is a sublessee, his/her attorney should receive and review the underlying, or master, lease on the franchisee's behalf. The purpose for this is to make the franchisee aware of the restrictions and obligations contained within. By reviewing the master lease, the franchisee will be able to determine the amount of rent the lease calls for, then pay that amount, or slightly more for an administrative fee for the franchisor to handle the rental payment. Once the franchisee has seen the master lease, he/she protects him/herself against rent scalping—the practice of the franchisor hiking up the rent and creating a profit center for itself.

Making a standard security deposit payment to the lessor may be one way of both relieving the franchisor from giving a guarantee and the franchisee from having to pay for it.

If the franchisor is the sublessor, the franchisor may be required to give the lessor a financial guarantee that the rent will be timely paid. There may be an attempt by the franchisor to charge for this guarantee. If possible, avoid compensating the franchisor. Making a standard security deposit payment to the lessor may be one way of both relieving the franchisor from giving a guarantee and the franchise from having to pay for it. Never offer more than two months rent as security deposit.

When the franchisee is a sublessee, there is always the possibility that he/she can be evicted. The franchisor may fail to renew the lease by not exercising an option, allowing the notice period to pass, or failing to pay the rent. The best way to remedy the latter is to insist on paying rent directly to the lessor. Further, if the franchisee can negotiate the ability to exercise an option to renew the lease in the event the franchisor fails to do so, he/she will protect his/her investment in that location. Provided the franchisee complies with the lease and the sublease, eviction should not be a possibility.

The Contract Phase

Unless the franchisee purchased an existing franchise and inherited the transferor's lease, which may prevent any changes, the leasing experience begins with the contract phase. This is a period of time when the franchisee, the broker and possibly the franchisor have expressed interest in leasing a specific piece of property. In many cases, the business terms of the lease will be worked out before a letter of intent is drafted. Once the letter of intent is drafted, setting forth the key terms, the lessor customarily prepares a lease implementing the business terms. As noted the lease can be expected to weigh heavily in favor of the lessor. At this point, the franchisee's lawyer should carefully review the lease. Abstracting the lease is usually a good idea for future discussions with clients and the lessor's representatives. Since most leases are long, standard documents, an abstract—a detailed, annotated outline—will assist the lawyer's memory when meeting with clients and can be a valuable tool to point out those sections the lawyer suggests be amended, modified or deleted.

The contracting process is the most important part of leasing. If the franchisee negotiates a good contract, with fair rent, he/she may preclude problems from arising in the future. The franchisee's lawyer should be familiar with the franchise agreement and incorporate the lease provisions required of the franchisor or the particular franchise. This includes understanding the way in which the franchise agreement and the lease work together and how the default of one could mean the unjustified, but valid, termination of the other.

> *Unlike many franchise agreements which franchisors refuse to change, leases must be tailored to the specific use for which they are executed.*

The contract phase is the best, and possibly only, time a lessee will have to propose changes. Clearly, once the lease is signed, few lessors will entertain changes. Unlike many franchise agreements which franchisors refuse to change, leases must be tailored to the specific use for which they are executed. Based on the type of premises, the type of franchise, the term involved, the delay in rental commencement, the build-out allowance, the security deposit and other terms and conditions, leases should not be the same for any two tenants. Many more variables promote changing a lease than a franchise agreement, which tends to be standard for each franchisee. For example, the franchisee should try to get the term of the lease to be exactly the same as the term of the franchise agreement.

Negotiation

In assessing the possibilities for negotiation, the franchisee's attorney should review, among others factors, the amount of time the property has been on the market, whether the square foot cost has dropped since the property was listed, the condition of the premises (how much work must the franchisee do before the premises are suitable for operating the franchise), whether a build-on allowance has been provided and the age of the lessor's equipment—such as heating and air conditioning units. It is important to know the values in the market in order to compare the subject property with like property. The franchisee's attorney must be able to relate various terms of the lease to the particulars of the franchise—such as hours of operation, signage and trademark usage—and make an argument for the inclusion or exclusion of certain clauses, based on their applicability to the franchise.

> *To limit competition, an exclusivity provision could be suggested.*

The View from the Franchisee Side

When negotiating a lease, certain provisions should be uppermost in the franchisee's lawyer's mind. To limit competition, an exclusivity provision should be suggested. Unfettered ability to assign the lease to a transferee franchisee should also be proposed. The justification for this right is the franchisor's screening and qualification process. However, experience shows lessors prefer to control who comes into their space, regardless of the criteria and the selection process used by franchisors. Lessors will sometimes amend such a provision to state that if the incoming franchisee can show a net worth equal to or greater than the selling franchisee, the lessor will be more inclined to approve the incoming franchisee. More often than not, this control mechanism is retained.

> *Don't sign a lease if the lessor will not support the CAM and taxes with hard numbers.*

There are other important do's and don'ts when negotiating the lease. If percentage rent is written into the lease, it should be deleted. If that is not possible, the revenue barrier should be raised as high as possible. A lessee should never agree to a confession of judgment or to waive the right to trial by jury. A lessee must have an option to automatically renew the lease once proper notice is given. A franchisee should not sign a lease without a renewal; it severely limits the franchisee. If it is necessary to go back to the lessor at the end of the lease and request a new lease, the new may be less favorable. Further, the lessee is in a very vulnerable position since he/she has expressed a desire to stay and maintain continuity in the business. The lessor must offer to open the books to the lessee to verify CAM and taxes. He/she should not sign a lease if the lessor will not support the CAM and taxes with hard numbers. The lease must let the franchisee, subject to municipal code, put up the sign approved by the franchisor which displays the franchisor's trademark. A franchisee must think twice about signing a lease for a location forcing conformity to the shopping center's monotone, single line, same size signs. He/she should not sign a lease if it gives permission to the lessor to terminate the lease if the lessee requests the right to transfer or assign. That lease has effectively cut off the ability to sell a franchise at that location with confidence that the purchaser will be able to operate out of those premises.

Additionally, and also by way of example, he/she should not sign a lease if the lease precludes ownership of another system's franchises within a specific measured radius or if it requires the lessee to pay a percentage of those sales to the lessor. Two things can happen in a situation like that. First, the lessee can be precluded from taking advantage of a good site, which may present itself within that distance, and second, he/she may not be able to limit competition by purchasing that second site. This can result in sharing the market with a fellow franchisee, thus decreasing market share and making advertising less effective.

Condition of Premises

The condition is important since it determines how much money a lessee will be required to spend to meet the franchisor's requirements. There are various presentations, such as *vanilla boxes,* which could mean the premises are given possession, without any build-out. Sometimes the walls are painted, other times the lessee starts with totally unfinished space. The lessor could contract with the lessee to build out the space, which can be paid for up front or during a period of time during over which he/she occupies the space. If the lessor builds out space, he/she should get specific time frames for completion, since this will impact the franchise's opening. Frequently, a lessor's work letter will be attached to the lease as an exhibit. If there is none, he/she should ask for one. The lessee may be required to hire a general contractor and build out the space. In this case, he/she should get a fair idea as to when the job can be completed since rent will presumably be paid during the build-out. The condition of the premises may also be a bargaining chip when negotiating the rent.

Heating, Ventilation and Air Conditioning

As a lessee, the franchisee will probably be required to maintain the HVAC system and replace it if it malfunctions.

When investigating a location, the franchisee must make certain inspections and gather information about specific operating systems. Among these will be the inspection of the heating, ventilation and air conditioning system, commonly referred to as HVAC. The HVAC will control the temperature in the premises throughout the year. As a lessee, the franchisee will probably be required to maintain the system and replace it if it malfunctions. As a result, he/she will want to know going in what this unit looks like.

In most instances the franchisee will be unable to test both the heating and the air conditioning systems. A good test of the air conditioning system can only take place when the temperature is 70 degrees or higher, when the compressor kicks on. If the leasing search takes place in November in the Midwest, this will be impossible. A clause should be written into the lease that as soon as the air conditioning unit can be tested, a licensed air conditioning and heating professional will be retained to test it. If it is defective, the lessor will accommodate the lessee by either outright fixing it or, if need be, replacing the entire unit. The same arrangement should be made for the heating if the inspection takes place in the summer.

Although this may sound like common sense, many franchisees have spent years complaining about the effect these systems have had on their businesses. Take an ice cream store that does not have adequate ventilation and air conditioning. The heat generated by the freezers can take its toll and cause the product to melt. This is an extreme example. However, any location which cannot properly control its temperature will lose customers. The loss of customers for franchisees means lower profits. If this can be prevented by adequate inspections before signing a lease, the time and money should be spent to do so. These systems also must be assured of meeting local safety, fire and building codes.

Environmental Considerations

It is recommended that indemnification language be negotiated to protect the franchisee to the greatest extent possible.

There is no practical reason a franchisee leasing a location should ever assume an environmental risk. The lease should be written such that the lessor completely indemnifies the franchisee from any and all environmental problems up to the date the franchisee takes possession. Further, and depending on the type of business, if the franchisee does not use, store or work with any hazardous materials, there should be a further provision stating if a problem occurs during the lease term, the franchisee will not be responsible. The latter is difficult to secure, since the only way a problem can occur when a franchisee does not have contact with hazardous materials is through migration. If migration occurs, it can be very difficult to trace the origin of a leak. Lessors are reluctant to provide these blanket indemnifications, but due to the cost of a clean-up or redemption, it is recommended that indemnification language be negotiated to protect the franchisee to the greatest extent possible.

Signage and Hours

Unlike rent, security deposit, repairs and various other factors over which the franchisor has no input, signage, hours and insurance are three of the more important issues, where franchise and lease requirements may conflict.

Signage requirements are extremely important for franchised businesses. Presumably, the franchisor will dictate size, color, type, etc. Likewise, lessors may require conformity with shopping center designs and may limit the size and type of letters, the colors and the height, etc. Restrictions on signs affect uniformity and franchise identity, ultimately costing sales. Additionally, the municipality in which the premises are located may dictate the final sign requirements.

When considering signage requirements, franchisees must be aware of the following:

- Placement of and the type of sign represent one set of issues.
- Removal of signs and their ownership after the lease expires represent a second set of issues.
- Proper use of the trademark as used in signage represents a third set of issues.

Negotiating the proper amount of hours for the specific type of franchise is very important.

Uniform hours help control the uniformity of the franchise. Lessors may require a variance to comply with the hours of the other lessees. Negotiating the proper amount of hours for the specific type of franchise is very important.

Insurance

There are various types of insurance available to commercial businesses, including, but not limited to general liability, casualty, business interruption, plate glass, owned and non-owned vehicles, etc. The franchisor frequently includes the types of insurance required for operating the franchise. In addition, the franchisee must be aware of the following, all or some of which may be prescribed by the franchisor:

- **Deductibles**—Amounts paid by the insured before the insurance coverage applies.
- **Additional Insured**—other parties such as the lessor and the franchisor.
- **Indemnification**—the promise to prevent another party from incurring any losses.
- **Subrogation**—the understanding that one party can collect in place of another.

Assignment and Sublease

Whenever an assignment has taken place, the franchisee's lawyer should do whatever is necessary to bring about an end to the relationship between the lessor and the client.

There are fundamental differences between an assignment and the sublease of real property. An assignment means that a lessee assigns his/her lease to a third party, who then deals with the lessor directly. Depending on the strength of the third party, the original lessee may be removed from lease all together. Whenever an assignment has taken place, the franchisee's lawyer should do whatever is necessary to bring about an end to the relationship between the lessor and the client.

On the other hand, a sublease means that the lessee has let or leased part or all of his/her premises to a third party, who enters into a contract for all or a portion of the remainder of the term. The lessor will not let the original lessee off the lease at that point, as he/she will be an essential guarantor throughout the term of the lease. As a sublessor, the original lessee may have to collect rent, then remit it to the lessor.

Zoning and Permits

The franchisee must ascertain whether the premises in which its franchise operation will take place is zoned for that activity, and if not, how quickly a special use permit will be issued. Although zoning issues should be dealt with before serious leasing negotiations begin, sometimes they are overlooked. This can result in added expense and possible forfeiture of the location. Once the lease has been negotiated, the process to receive a permit may take much longer than anticipated. Franchisees who must open to take advantage of a specific season should pay careful attention to this factor. Inspections by local government agents are usually unavoidable—but still useful—so ask for one and get it done early so it will highlight any problems before a commitment is made.

> *The quicker one can be relieved of a personal guarantee, the better.*

Guarantors

From the franchisee standpoint, the best guarantor is none at all. Franchisees are encouraged to sign leases in the name of the franchisee's corporation, not in their personal names. Certain lessors will assess the amount of assets within the franchisee's corporation and make a determination as to whether or not there is sufficient coverage. If there is insufficient coverage, and the lessor requires a higher comfort level, the individual shareholders will be required to personally guarantee the lease. It is recommended that this be avoided, if possible. If not, the franchisee's attorney must try to negotiate kick-out or buy-out clauses. Additionally, a proposal can be made that, after a set period of time, the guarantee will no longer be necessary. Another possibility is to propose a short-term letter of credit for an amount that may cover one, or at the most two years, of the lease. There are plusses and minuses to each of these. Suffice it to say, the quicker one can be relieved of a personal guarantee, the better.

Cross Defaults

Cross defaults result when a default in one agreement causes an automatic default in another agreement with the same party.

Cross defaults result when a default in one agreement causes an automatic default in another agreement with the same party. For example, the failure to pay the rent may provide a reason to terminate both the lease and the franchise agreement. A cross default can be totally unjustified, since there are many reasons that a lessee or sublessee may not pay rent. Nevertheless, if the franchise is a party to more than one agreement with the franchisor, the agreements should be carefully reviewed to determine if there are cross default provisions. The franchisee should always try very hard to eliminate any cross default clauses.

This chapter has touched on many of the areas a franchisee lessee will encounter in the leasing process. Following this advice will give franchisees stronger leases and help prevent the lessor, or the franchisor sublessor, from taking unfair advantage of him/her. Knowing how to integrate and coordinate the franchise agreement with the lease is very important, too. A sensible approach to leasing a location at which the franchisee will operate is to hire a knowledgeable attorney who is not afraid to submit a substantial amendment and fight for changes, even if it means going back two or three times. This kind of effort can go a long way. Just as franchise agreements can be amended, leases can be subject to modifications which can benefit franchisees.

Estate Planning Issues

Estate planning can have a significant effect on the transfer of a franchised business upon the death of an individual franchisee.

Estate planning is generally an area that is overlooked by individuals, whether or not they are franchisees. Estate planning can have a significant effect on the transfer of a franchise business upon the death of an individual franchisee. It can also have an effect on the general estate plan of the individual, since most businesses have a *value (goodwill)* which needs to be incorporated into the overall estate plan valuation process. Even though the issue of goodwill in a franchise is a subject of much debate, there is a certain value that can be placed on that franchise as a going concern and, therefore, must be evaluated with other estate planning assets. In evaluating an estate plan, there are many tax planning considerations that go into the process. There are also other issues, such as, the uninterrupted continuation of the business after death so that heirs and/or beneficiaries will be able to receive the benefits of the business/franchise. Peculiar to franchising, many franchise agreements have provisions concerning the death of an individual franchisee. The provisions may provide for the automatic transfer to a spouse or child without losing the value of the business, the sale of the franchise to a qualified franchisee by the estate or the outright purchase of the franchise by the franchisor, or by right of first refusal.

The estate planning process should begin when entering into a franchise agreement and with forming the entity to operate the franchise. There may be estate planning concerns that should be incorporated into a partnership, shareholder or operating agreement. It is important to have an attorney at the very least, discuss these issues. For another example, a franchisee's lawyer may advise that the franchise agreement be transferred into and owned by a trust that controls what happens to the asset if he/she dies or becomes disabled.

An estate plan allows an individual to determine how his/her assets will be distributed, whether it is a small or large estate.

The estate planning process is not just for the wealthy. Contrary to this misconception, an estate plan is necessary for everybody. An estate plan allows an individual to determine how his/her assets will be distributed, whether it is a small or large estate. Without a will, state law will govern disbursement of those assets.

Another document typically utilized in forming an estate plan is a *power of attorney*, which allows for someone else to step in and to act in the event of certain situations, like disability. The final document used is sometimes referred to as a *living will* or *advanced health care directive*, which authorizes medical personnel not to administer certain medical procedures.

Everyone should have his/her estate reviewed, if for no other reason, so that he/she instead of the courts, can appoint a guardian for minor children should both parents be deceased. Estate plans are for everyone. There is no minimum dollar amount to qualify.

Employment Issues

Contract vs. At-Will Employment

Many estates recognize *at-will* employment. That is to say that the courts presume that employment is at the will of either party. The employee may leave at any time; the employer may terminate an employee at any time, for any reason or no reason. However, an employer may not terminate for an illegal reason.

The exception to at-will employment is created by a contract (oral or written) for a definite period of time. A contract of employment *for life* is generally unenforceable. Only upon establishing a contract of employment for a definite period of time may an employee avoid the at-will employment presumption. Conversely, if a contract of employment provides that employment is at will, then the employee is bound by such a contractual provision.

Courts have recognized a fraudulent inducement argument. For example, if an employee specifically asks if a prospective employer is about to go through a merger and is told directly that there are no expectations of merger, when in fact there are, the employee may have a claim for wrongful termination following a merger.

Wrongful Discharge/Termination

Certain states recognize a claim for wrongful discharge of an at-will employee, only where the discharge would be in violation of public policy. Public policy is generally found only where there is a statute defining the policies at issue. For example, an employee may have a claim for wrongful discharge if he/she reports for jury duty despite the employer's instructions not to do so. However, such claims are extremely difficult to prove, and the burden on the employee is great.

An employee charging sexual harassment must be able to prove that the employer was aware of the conduct and failed to take any action to prevent it.

In sexual harassment situations, there is no automatic liability on the part of the employer for *hostile environment* types of claims, but an employer likely *will* be automatically liable for so-called *quid-pro-quo* sexual harassment, where job benefits, promotions or demotions depend on the employee providing sexual favors to a supervisor.

An employee charging *hostile environment* sexual harassment must be able to prove that the employer was aware of the conduct and failed to take any action to prevent it. An employer can generally protect him/herself from a claim of *hostile environment* sexual harassment by having in place a written policy prohibiting such conduct and providing for procedures whereby employees can report such activity directly to a high-level supervisor. In this fashion, the employee can be prevented from claiming that the immediate supervisor was the person permitting the illegal harassment. One means of creating employer liability is to show that the person engaging in the illegal sexual harassment is the employer—that is to say, a high level owner/manager. The rules regarding sexual harassment generally apply to racial discrimination as well.

On the issue of privacy, many states recognize a right of privacy and a violation of that right as an actionable tort. An action for invasion of privacy is comprised of four distinct torts:

- intrusion upon seclusion,
- appropriation of name or likeness,
- publicity given to private life and
- publicity placing the person in a false light.

A urine-testing program might constitute an invasion of privacy if the testing revealed medical conditions in addition to the presence of drugs.

The first of these is of concern regarding searches of employees and vehicles. One who intentionally intrudes, physically or otherwise, upon the solitude or seclusion of another or his/her private affairs or concerns, is subject to liability to the other for invasion of his/her privacy, if the intrusion would be highly offensive to a reasonable person. In an employment context, it has been held that the opening of mail directed to an employee and marked *confidential* is an invasion of privacy. A urine-testing program might constitute an invasion of privacy if the testing revealed medical conditions in addition to the presence of drugs. An observer in a bathroom of an employee giving a urine sample is indiscreet and an invasion of privacy.

ADA and FMLA

The Americans with Disabilities Act (ADA) prohibits employment discrimination against a qualified individual because of a disability. An employer is required to make reasonable accommodations to the known physical or mental limitations of an otherwise qualified individual who is an applicant or employee, unless the employer can demonstrate that the accommodation would impose an undue hardship on the operation of its business. Much litigation surrounds whether an individual is *qualified* in spite of his or her disability; as well as what accommodations are *reasonable* and what constitutes an *undue hardship*. Fundamentally, an employee must be able to come to work and do a job. As in so many other areas of regulations, a franchisee must get expert legal advice when dealing with ADA issues. And the ADA also requires full handicap accessibility to your facilities for guests, vendors and employees.

The Family Medical Leave Act (FMLA) requires an employer to provide an employee 12 work weeks of leave during any twelve month period for the birth of a child of the employee, in order to care for such child; for the placement of a son or daughter with the employee for adoption or foster case; the caring for the spouse, son, daughter or parent of the employee if they have a serious health condition; and of a serious health condition that makes the employee unable to perform the functions of his or her position. The FMLA provides for certain conditions in regard to the taking of leave. The employer is not required to pay the employee during such leave. The employer can require certification in regard to a serious health condition. The FMLA requires the employer to restore the employee to the position of employment held when the leave commenced, or to an equivalent position with equivalent employment benefits, pay and other terms and conditions.

Unemployment Compensation

The fundamental question in determining whether an employee is entitled to unemployment compensation is: Did the employee engage in *willful misconduct*? If an employee is terminated for willful misconduct, he or she may not receive unemployment compensation. On the other hand, if there is no willful misconduct, the employee is generally entitled to such compensation. Unemployment compensation referees and the courts have a general tendency to award compensation in a close case.

Employee Handbooks

*An employee handbook can establish
clear rules for the employee to follow.*

An employee handbook can be a very good tool for an employer. An employee handbook can establish clear rules for the employee to follow. On the other hand, an employee handbook can be construed as a contract in terms of benefits and conditions of employment. An employee handbook is not generally considered a contract of employment sufficient to remove the presumption of at-will employment. Nonetheless, any employee handbook should have clear language stating that it does not affect at-will employment.

Should a franchisee create an employee handbook, he/she should take care to revise it upon any change in benefits or conditions of employment. If there are no written changes to the employee handbook, a court could find that the employer bound to pay benefits and follow conditions in the written handbook, which had not been updated.

CHAPTER VI
Advertising Fund Agreements

Advertising and marketing funds are universally recognized as a quintessential part of most franchise relationships. A franchise necessarily involves a trademark or trade name. Through a number of properties/outlets, whether company-owned or franchisee-owned, a sizable pool of money can be collected for the franchise system to engage in significant advertising and promotion campaigns. Such advertising and promotional efforts may include regional or national print, radio and television advertising and various public relations activities which would be prohibitively expensive for individual, or even small groups, of franchisees.

Advertising fund agreements are invariably the subject of written contract provisions. Sometimes the advertising or marketing fund provisions are included in the basic franchise agreement. In other franchise systems, the advertising funds are the subject of a separate or collateral agreement.

Ad fund agreement provisions typically include some or all of the following provisions:

- Who controls the ad fund (usually either the franchisor or a new separate entity)?
- How much are the ad fund contributions (usually a percentage of gross sales)?
- What will the money be spent on?
- Can the franchisor charge its own overhead costs against the franchisees' advertising fund?
- Where will the money be spent?

- Who decides upon what the ad fund money will be deployed?
- What accountability is provided for the administration of the funds and their investment or use?

Overview on the Law of Fiduciary Duties

The term fiduciary connotes a special relationship of great trust as between a bank holding funds for widows and orphans.

The term fiduciary, is defined by *Black's Law Dictionary* as follows: "The term is derived from the Roman law, and means (as a noun) a person holding the character of a trustee, or a character analogous to that of a trustee, in respect to the trust and confidence involved in it and the scrupulous good faith and candor which it requires." The term fiduciary connotes a special relationship of great trust as between a bank holding funds for widows and orphans. Indeed, most American courts have treated certain relationships as automatically creating fiduciary relationships, including attorney-client, bank-deposit holder, conservator-conservatee, insurer-insured, principal-agent and trustee-beneficiary. A common thread in these relationships is that complete trust is imposed on the beneficiary by the fiduciary who is usually unable to protect his or her own interest.

Most courts have recognized fiduciary relationships when a significant level of trust over one's property is placed in another.

Outside of the above, well-recognized areas of fiduciary relationships, most courts have recognized fiduciary relationships when a significant level of trust over one's property is placed in another. Whether such a level of trust exists outside a per se fiduciary relationship is usually a question of fact. When a sufficient level of trust does not exist, while the parties may have ordinary contractual duties, a fiduciary duty will not exist. Most, but not all, courts which have reviewed facts regarding particular franchisor-franchisee relationships have not found a fiduciary duty.

Broussard v. Meineke Discount Muffler Shops, Inc.

One of the most successful cases on advertising funds was the *Meineke* case. The franchisees sued the franchisor in a class action suit for advertising misconduct. At the trial the plaintiffs presented some of the following evidence.

- The ad fund was to be maintained as a separate trust fund account and managed for the benefit of the Meineke franchisees; however the defendant Meineke, to the contrary, managed the ad fund account for its own benefit.
- Defendent Meineke swept the ad funds into its own accounts so that they earned interest for Meineke at the expense of the ad fund.
- Defendant Meineke withdrew ad fund monies to settle lawsuits.
- Defendant Meineke used ad fund monies to pay its own corporate expenses.
- Defendant Meineke also purchased superfluous advertising to generate advertising commission for itself.
- Defendant Meineke negotiated volume discounts for advertising but pocketed the difference for itself instead of giving the ad fund any discounts.
- Defendant Meineke used the ad fund monies to generate new franchisees instead of promoting business for existing franchisees.
- Defendant Meineke concealed its activities from its franchisees by false and misleading representations.

The trial courts affirmed the jury verdict for breach of fiduciary duty, breach of contract, fraud and violations of the North Carolina Unfair and Deceptive Practices Act. The fiduciary duty cause of action was possible due to specific promises made by defendant Meineke Muffler about the ad fund.

(Editor's Note: On August 19, 1998, the U.S. Court of Appeals for the Fourth District reversed *Broussard v. Meineke* in its entirety and remanded to the district court for further proceedings.)

Breach of Contract and Advertising Fund Agreements

As with franchise agreements, advertising fund contract provisions generally have been drafted with great care and precision to benefit franchisors over the years.

As with franchise agreements, advertising fund contract provisions generally have been drafted with great care and precision to benefit franchisors over the years. Many courts have upheld seemingly unfair or injudicious use of advertising funds when the contract provided for such expenditures. The starting point in analyzing a franchisor's advertising fund conduct is the contract language providing for the advertising or marketing fund.

In most franchise agreements, the franchisor is entitled to receive the advertising revenues and control the advertising fund.

In most franchise agreements, the franchisor is entitled to receive the advertising revenues and control the advertising fund. When an agreement provides for a separate trust or committee to control the advertising fund money, however, the franchisor cannot obtain and control the ad fund monies.

One common type of ad fund contract provision provides discretion over the use of advertising monies. As with cases interpreting the covenant of good faith and fair dealing, courts are split in interpreting such provisions. Some courts require the franchisor to exercise the discretion reasonably while other courts grant unfettered discretion and control to the franchisor.

In *America's Favorite Chicken Co. vs. Cajun Enterprises, Inc.,* the franchisor was granted *sole discretion* over the advertising funds. A group of California franchisees claimed, however, that sufficient advertising had not been done in California. They claimed the advertising centered on Louisiana, where the franchisor operated many units. Under Louisiana law, sole discretion over advertising allowed such decisions to be made by the franchisor. Thus, the franchisees' claims about where the advertising funds were spent were dismissed by summary judgment, and the court of appeals decision was affirmed.

In contrast, in *Burger King Corp. vs. Austin,* a claim of breach of the covenant of good faith and fair dealing was allowed to proceed. The franchisor reserved control as follows: "All [advertising, sales promotion and public relations] expenditures shall be at the discretion of BKC." Despite this language, the court held that the franchisor had to exercise discretion consistent with the parties' reasonable expectations.

Breach of Covenant of Good Faith and Fair Dealing and Advertising Funds

The covenant of good faith and fair dealing is also useful regarding advertising funds.

One of the franchisees' most powerful sources of relief is the covenant of good faith and fair dealing implicit in every agreement. The covenant of good faith and fair dealing is also useful for franchisees regarding advertising funds.

Most courts apply three general concepts regarding the covenant of good faith and fair dealing. First, the covenant requires that one party not undertake actions to deprive the other party of the benefits or reasonable expectations under the agreement. Second, when one party is vested with discretion, even sole discretion, that party may not unreasonably exercise that discretion. Finally, the covenant will not be used to override express terms of the agreement.

Breach of Fiduciary Duty and Ad Fund Agreements

Arnott v. Amoco, CCH Para. 1,620.30, 609 F.2d 873 (8th Cir. 1974) (fiduciary duty).

Bain v. Champlin Petroleum Co., CCH Para. 7,861 (8th Cir. 1982) (no fiduciary duty; overruled Arnott).

Bonfield v. AAMCO Transmission, Inc., CCH Para. 9,469 (N.D. I11. 1989) (no fiduciary).

Burger King Corp. v. Austin, CCH Para. 10,104 (S.D.Fla. 1992) (no fiduciary duty).

Carter Equipment Co. v. John Deere Industrial Equipment Co., CCH Para. 7,859 (5th Cir. 1982). (Question of fact regarding fiduciary duty between franchisor and franchisee).

Oil Express National, Inc. V. Burgstone, CCH Para. 11,148 (N.D. I11. 1997) (no fiduciary duty, but some other claims).

Thompson v. Atlantic Richfield Co., CCH Para. 9,048 (W.D. Wash. 1987) (no trust relationship).

Fraud and Ad Fund Agreements

It may be possible to attack a franchisor's conduct with respect to the advertising fund on the basis of fraud. If a franchisor has represented (either in the franchise agreement or orally) that collected ad funds will be spent for certain purposes and that the franchisor will not skim off part of the fund to pay its own overhead, such actions might well be attacked as fraudulent promises.

In most jurisdictions, fraud is:

- A false representation or omission of a material fact
- Reasonably calculated to deceive
- Made with intent to deceive
- Which does in fact deceive the plaintiff, and
- Which results in damages to the injured party.

Thus, where the franchisor has committed improper acts with the fund, it may be possible to allege that the franchisor intended, right from the beginning, to take the actions it did. That is, when the franchisor made *representations* in the franchise agreement and/or the circular about how the fund was going to spent and administered, the franchisor commits fraud if it subsequently does not handle the fund as represented.

The beauty of a fraud claim is that, if proved, punitive damages can be assessed against the defendant. While this admittedly does not happen very often in franchise litigation, it does happen from time to time, and the very prospect of it may well convince a franchisor to change its methods.

Advertising Funds and Unfair Practices Act

Most states have unfair practices act statutes, sometimes known as little FTC Acts.

Most states have unfair practices act statutes, sometimes known as little FTC Acts. See, e.g., Cal. Bus. & Pro. Code 17200 et seq.; North Carolina Unfair Trade Practices Act, N.C. Gen. Stat. Sec. 75-1.1. These statutes are very useful for attacking a wide variety of franchisor practices because the statutes generally state that illegal, deceptive or unfair acts committed in the practice of a business are unlawful. By and large, these statutes do not permit the plaintiff to recover damages, but do permit, in addition to injunctive relief, the remedies of restitution or disgorgement.

Unfair practices act statutes can be used by a group of franchisees, or a franchisee association acting on behalf of its members, to attack the types of expenditures made by a franchisor from the fund and, particularly, payments from the fund to the franchisor itself for *administrative expenses.* Upon proof that a franchisor has committed an illegal or *unfair* act with regard to the fund, the franchisor can be made to pay back into the fund whatever has been taken out for the improper expenditure or payment.

Other Issues and Ad Fund Agreements

Doctor's Associates, Inc. v. Hollingsworth, CCH Para. 11069 (D. Conn. 1996). Franchisees filed a class action, not against the franchisor, but against the Subway Franchisees Advertising

Trust Fund, its executive director and the individual owners of
the franchisor. Noting that the franchise agreements contained
an arbitration clause, the court stayed the litigation and forced
the franchisees into arbitration on the grounds that the claims
were related to the franchise agreements, which contained
mandatory arbitration clauses.

Afterword

It is my sincere hope that the learnings in this book have been valuable for the reader. The serious, conscientious and astute businessperson who incorporates these tools into their next franchise negotiation can consider themselves, if not a step ahead of their franchisor, then at least on the same page.

I hope too, that franchisors who read this book will be motivated to be more reasonable, factual and fair in their dealings with their franchisees. There is nothing written in franchising that says one party must thrive at the expense of the other party. That's the old win-lose scenario. We're looking for a win-win. And as a result, both parties can prosper in their endeavors.

Jay S. Patel
President and CEO
Lodging Hospitality Systems, Inc.
September 1999

The following is an alphabetical listing of experienced franchise attorneys. Except where indicated, these attorneys are Affiliate Members of the American Franchisee Association (AFA).

Brent R. Appel, Esq.
Dickinson, Mackman, Tyler & Hagan, P.C.
699 Walnut Street, Suite 1600   Tel.: 515-246-4549
Des Moines, IA 50309   Fax: 515-246-4554

Hitendra Bhakta, Esq.**
Law Office of Norman Filer
500 N. State Blvd.
Suite 1270   Tel.: 714- 634-1717
Orange, CA 92868   Fax: 714-634-2855

Theodore Becker, Esq.
Becker & Kaplan, L.L.C.
19 S. LaSalle St., Ste. 1500   Tel.: 312-621-9500
Chicago, IL 60603   Fax: 312-621-9011

Marc N. Blumenthal, Esq.
Law Office of Marc N. Blumenthal
19 S. LaSalle St., Suite 1500   Tel.: 312-641-0616
Chicago, IL 60603   Fax: 312-332-4629

Donald D. Boroian, Chairman/CEO   **(Expert Witness)**
Francorp
20200 Governors Drive, Suite 300   Tel.: 708-481-2900
Olympia Fields, IL 60461   Fax: 708-481-5885

**Not an AFA Affiliate Member.

Howard Bundy, Esq.
Bundy & Morrill, Inc., P.S.
12351 Lake City Way NE, Ste. 202   Tel.: 206-367-4640
Seattle, WA 98125   Fax: 206-367-5507

Patrick Carter, Esq.
Law Offices of Patrick J. Carter
44 Montgomery Street, Ste. 4210   Tel.: 415-433-1025
San Francisco, CA 94194   Fax: 415-433-0451

Carmen D. Caruso, Esq.
Carmen D. Caruso, P.C.
10 S. LaSalle St., Ste. 3500   Tel.: 312-920-0160
Chicago, IL 60603   Fax: 312-920-0162

Harris J. Chernow, Esq.
Heller, Kapustin, Gershman & Vogel, P.C.
486 Norristown Road, Ste. 230   Tel.: 610-825-3600
Blue Bell, PA 19422   Fax: 610-834-7737

New Jersey Office:
Temar Plaza, Ste. 112
20 Brace Road   Tel.: 856-616-9193
Cherry Hill, NJ 08034   Fax: 856-667-4336

South Carolina (Affiliated) Office:
1634 Main Street, Ste. 200
PO Box 72   Tel.: 803-256-9664
Columbia, SC 29202   Fax: 803-256-3056

Michael Dady, Esq.
Dady & Garner, P.A.
400 IDS Center
80 South Eight St.   Tel.: 612-359-3500
Minneapolis, MN 55402   Fax: 612-359-3507

Michael Einbinder, Esq.
Rosen, Einbinder & Dunn. P.C.
641 Lexington Ave.   Tel.: 212-888-7717
New York, NY 10022   Fax: 212-980-1444

Jeffery M. Goldstein, Esq. *
Birch, Horton, Bittner & Cherot
1155 Connecticut Avenue, NW   Tel.: 202-659-5800
Washington, DC 20036   Fax: 202-659-1027

Eric H. Karp, Esq.
Witmer, Karp, Warner & Thuotte, L.L.P.
28 State St.   Tel.: 617-248-0550
Boston, MA 02109   Fax: 617-248-0607

Peter C. Lagarias, Esq.
The Legal Solutions Group, L.L.P.
1629 5th Ave.   Tel.: 415-460-0100
San Rafael, CA 94901   Fax: 415-460-1099

Wayne Lazarus, Esq.***
Stokes, Lazarus & Carmichael, L.L.P.
80 Peachtree Park Dr., NE   Tel.: 404-352-1465
Atlanta, GA 30309   Fax: 404-352-8463

Michael R. Liss, Esq.
FRANLAW: Davis, Hands & Liss
1301 West 22nd St., Ste. 615   Tel.: 630-325-6545
Oak Brook, IL 60523   Fax: 630-574-0319

Gerald A. Marks, Esq.
Marks & Krantz
63 Riverside Ave.   Tel.: 732-747-7100
Red Bank, NJ 07701   Fax: 732-219-0625

**Not an AFA Affiliate Member.
***AAHOA Affiliated Attorney who is not an AFA Affiliate Member.

Christopher McElgunn, Esq.
Klenda, Mitchell, Austerman & Zuercher, L.L.C.
1600 Epic Center
310 N. Main   Tel.: 316-267-0331
Wichita, KS 67202   Fax: 316-267-0333

Himanshu Patel, Esq.
Zarco & Pardo
One International Place
100 S. East 2nd Street, 27th Floor   Tel.: 305-374-5418
Miami, FL 33131   Fax: 305-374-5428
Email: zarcopardo@zarcopardo.com

Shawn Perry, Esq.
Perry, Perry & Perry
402 Towle Building
330 2nd Ave. South   Tel.: 612-332-8100
Minneapolis, MN 55401   Fax: 612-332-8166

Kenneth A. Rutherford, Esq.
The Rutherford Law Firm
PO Box 1381   Tel.: 662-513-3901
Oxford, MS 38655   Fax: 662-513-3904

Andy Selden, Esq.***
Briggs & Morgan, P.A.
2400 IDS Center
80 South 8th St.   Tel.: 612-334-8485
Minneapolis, MN 55402   Fax: 612-334-8650

Peter Singler, Jr., Esq.
Law Offices of Peter J. Singler. Jr.
6950 Burnett St., Ste. 200   Tel.: 707-823-8719
Sebastopol, CA 95472   Fax: 707-823-8737

**Not an AFA Affiliate Member.
***AAHOA Affiliated Attorney who is not an AFA Affiliate Member.

Joseph Thomson, Esq.
Lindquist & Vennum, P.L.L.P.
4200 IDS Center
80 South Eighth St.   Tel.: 612-371-3239
Minneapolis, MN 55402   Fax: 612-371-3207

Robert Zarco, Esq.
Zarco & Pardo, P.A.
Nationsbank at International Place
100 SE 2nd St., Ste. 2700   Tel.: 305-374-5418
Miami, FL 33131   Fax: 305-374-5428

About the Author

Jay S. Patel, CHA, cuts with either side of the franchising sword, both as a franchisee and franchisor. Patel is President/CEO of Lodging Hospitality Systems, Inc., (LHS) a franchise hotel company which franchises the Ashbury Suites & Inns concept as well as Chairman of the Board for Lodging Hospitality Hotels, Inc. (LHH), who owns and manages numerous nationally flagged properties. He brings this unique perspective and years of experience into the writing of *Franchising: Is It Fair?, "How to Negotiate an Equitable Franchise Agreement."*

Besides his 15 years of hotel management and development experience, Patel supports his book with numerous franchise industry experts. He has compiled the input of more than 15 experienced franchise attorneys from around the country, the American Franchisee Association (AFA) and the Asian American Hotel Owners Association (AAHOA) Board of Directors and the Industry Relations Committee.

Patel has served on the Board of Directors of the Indo-American Hospitality Association (IAHA) for several years until its merger with AAHOA in December of 1994. He has been Board representative for AAHOA to the American Franchisee Association (AFA) for the past several years and is an elected Delegate to the White House Conference on Small Business (WHCSB). Patel is also appointed to the Northern Florida District Small Business Administration (SBA) Advisory Council.

He lives in Pensacola, Florida, with his wife, two children and his mother. Patel has many accredits and recognitions to his name including being the recipient of the 1998 AAHOA Award of Excellence.